SCOTIA: LOST SISTER

CW01511413

"A modern exploration inspired by
century antiquarians and early Iri
book provides more convincing de
Egyptian princess Scota than one
An interesting read."
**ELLEN EVERT HOPMAN, author of "Celtic Druidry – Rituals,
Techniques and Magical Practices", "A Legacy of Druids –
Conversations with Druid leaders of Britain, the USA and
Canada, Past and Present", and of other volumes**

"Luke Eastwood's latest book is an intellectually honest, rigorous,
and erudite comparative analysis of the Scotia's story. Eastwood
has brought together a variety of sources which makes for a
compelling, enlightening, and highly recommended read."
**DR RACHEL SCOAZEC (PhD Irish Studies), Manager of
Kilderry Art, Nature and Tradition Centre, Kerry**

"Proof that ancient Egyptians came to Britain would change
human history. Great new evidence is now coming to light that
makes this theory possible. Read this extraordinary new book
and find out for yourself. A valuable new addition to the ancient
mysteries bookshelf."
**ANDREW COLLINS, author of "Author of Tutankhamun:
The Exodus Conspiracy" and Sobekneferu: The First Female
Pharaoh: Sobekneferu, Goddess of the Seven Stars"**

"There is nothing more wonderful than to witness the threads
of research weave together a picture of little known or obscure
historical figures. One such obscure figure is Scotia. Eastwood
leads the reader to Egypt, Spain, Scotland and Ireland through
his thorough research in an attempt to shine a spotlight on
Scotia. Despite the paucity of verifiable historical fact, the
reader is presented with in-depth historical contexts that
support the merging image and character of Scotia."
**PAULINE BREEN, author of "This is Brigid-Goddess & Saint",
"Maman Brigitte' and "Brigantia"**

"The true history of humanity has long been hidden from us. Thanks to the resilient work of inspired researchers and scholars, some important pieces of human history are being brought back to the surface, bringing clarity and understanding about our origins and the genetic links between different cultures on this planet. The links that can be traced back are sometimes quite remarkable. Did the ancient Egyptians make it to Scotland? And how does Tutankhamun fit in? Luke Eastwood lifts the veil on this fascinating but forgotten chapter of history. A highly recommended read."
ELENA DANAAN, author of "The Seeders"

If you love reading about ancient history... (the "this person is thought to have lived in 1356 BCE" kind of ancient) then this is the book for you. Eastwood's exploration of the royal line of Ancient Egypt is nothing short of heroic and he leaves no stone unturned in his literary archeologist efforts to research and convey the potential migration of Egyptians to Ireland and Scotland. In this book, one chapter builds on the next, so do not skip ahead. Information from the chapter you skip is necessary for following the (proposed) timeline of Meritaten's journey from Egypt to Spain to Scotland to Ireland. Since, as this book relates, 70% of British, Irish, and Spanish men and 50% of all Western European men are related to Tutankhamun, we know that Haplogroup R-M269 propagated there somehow. What started around the Black Sea 9500 years ago might well have pass through exactly the route and means the author proposes. My suggestion is to read the book and keep your mind open to the possibilities.
KATRINA RASBOLD, Editor of "Green Egg Magazine"

LUKE EASTWOOD was born in Scotland but he has lived in Ireland or England for most of his life. He is a graduate of City University, London. After a career as a recording artist he moved to Ireland in 1999. His first book *The Druid's Primer* was published in 2011 and this is his 11th book. Luke has been writing articles for magazines and websites since 1990. He is Managing Editor of Pagan Ireland magazine, since 2021. He lives in county Kerry, Ireland. **www.lukeeastwood.com**

SCOTIA

LOST SISTER OF TUTANKHAMUN

LUKE EASTWOOD

electric publications

In memory of Olivia Durdin-Robertson

First Published by Electric Publications, 2025

Electric Publications, Co. Kerry, Ireland
www.electricpublications.com

Unless otherwise stated:
Illustrations/Photographs copyright: Luke Eastwood 2025

Paperback ISBN: 978-1-7398625-2-7
Ebook ISBN: 978-1-7398625-3-4

A CIP catalogue record for this book is available from the British Library.

Edited, designed, printed and bound, in the Republic of Ireland

Printed by Modern Printers, Kilkenny, Ireland
modernprinters.ie

CONTENTS

ACKNOWLEDGEMENTS

Thanks to archaeologist Helana Zacharias, stone-mason Billy Lean, my co-author Gary Branigan (on Kerry Folk Tales), Declan, Celtic Studies expert Dr. Rachel Scoazec, John Knox, author Maureen Sullivan, Cyril Harrington and illustrator Elena Danann. A huge thanks to Steven Logan for bringing me to the Pharaoh exhibition in Melbourne. Thank you to author Ness Bosch for her invaluable assistance with Spanish information on Scotia and also to Professor Ramón Sainero (The Institute of Celtic Studies, UNED, Madrid) for his generous help. Thank you to Assistant Professor of Egyptology Francesco Tiradritti ("Kore" University of Enna) for his advice. Thanks also to author Jon G. Hughes and to Alex Robertson for their helpful advice. Thanks to authors Ellen Evert Hopman, Salicrow and Andrew Collins for their time and assistance. Thanks to Sally Robertson and Jane Evans for proof-reading. Thank you to archaeologist and author Lorraine Evans, whose work in this field has been invaluable, and for her frank and helpful suggestions. Thanks to my publishers and to all my friends and family that have supported my work.

Note: unless otherwise stated, all photographs and illustrations are by the author.

PREFACE

I was born in Scotland, in 1970, somewhere that at that time was in the depths of a financial recession and was a tough place to live. Ancient history, and history in general, was something for either tourists or academics - so Scotia was a name that was known to some, but it was a name that no-one ever mentioned. This may seem surprising, in a country that is literally named after this woman, but those were the times.

I first came across the name as a young man, perhaps at university, I am not really sure. My father knew a lot about Scottish history - Robert the Bruce, Bonnie Prince Charlie, the Stone of Scone etc, but I don't recall him ever mentioning Scotia/Scota. This name was just one of many of passing interest, that I half forgot about until I was in my early forties.

I heard the name mentioned in articles and videos, in relation to the Milesian invasion of Ireland and once again I saw it, in my reading of the 'Lebor Gabála Erenn' (Book of the Taking of Ireland), as part of research for my first book. While this was interesting, I did not expect Scotia to have any real impact on my own life, but I was quite wrong about that. Some years later, I met a French archaeologist who also shared an interest in Druidism and ancient history. It turned out that she had worked for the French Mission in Egypt for 9 years and had worked on or visited most of the major sites of Egyptian antiquity.

Over time she mentioned her travels and interesting events, including visiting empty tombs. At some point in our conversation the subject of Scotia came up, and she mentioned that Scotia had been an Egyptian Princess and a Queen for a short period of time. I was aware that Scotia had come from Spain, but I had not previously paid much attention to rumours of Scotia's Egyptian origins. My ears pricked up, I was curious to hear about the unused tomb of this woman, whose real name I learned for the first time - Meritaten.

At this time, I was not aware that a grave, attributed to Scotia, existed in the south-west of Ireland, not far from the town of Tralee, in county Kerry. I was intrigued to find out more about this mysterious Egyptian character and how she ended up living and dying in rainy Ireland. A few years later, I was able to visit the grave of Scotia, with the same French lady, which proved to be quite an experience. The place was very difficult to access due to the lack of paths and a series of rickety footbridges across the river, that took about 40 minutes to traverse. The site was quite impressive, but it seems it has never been excavated, which I found very surprising.

Not long after this first visit, I found myself moving to Kerry. A local project, in conjunction with Kerry County Council, to mark the existence of the grave of the mythical Scotia was underway. A local French lady, who is a painter and illustrator, was commissioned to design an obelisk with Kerry stone-mason Billy Lean. Having an understanding of Egyptian hieroglyphs, she was able to draw Scotia's Egyptian name for the obelisk, which Billy Lean carved for the installation in the small memorial garden created in the townland of Ballyard, some 5km from the actual burial site.

Ironically, I started a new job, shortly after this obelisk was erected and the fastest way to my then place of work was to drive right past it, every morning and evening. How strange it was then, when I was asked to co-write a book of stories about county Kerry ('Kerry Folk Tales') which would include Scotia. I agreed, of course. One of the stories on our list was the tale of Scotia and her demise in the county. I visited the site of Scotia's grave several more times, as it was barely more than a 30 minute drive from my home (plus a long walk), but at the time I had no idea that I would one day write an entire book about her.

A few years ago I decided to write a second book of stories, this time from just the Dingle peninsula, which I titled 'Dingle Folk Tales'. Seeing as Scotia's grave lies at the end of the Dingle peninsula, at the foot of the Sliabh Mish mountain range (that runs at least half-way across the middle of the peninsula), I thought it was appropriate to include her story. I completely rewrote the piece from the earlier book, a version that I did not feel was accurate enough, being basically a local legend. My new longer version I felt did Scotia justice, but still it only told the bare bones of her story.

Further conversations with my French source led to my own investigations into Scotia, and who she was before she arrived in Ireland. Without having met her, none of this would have happened in the first place. As I looked into this, I realised that no-one had ever put the entirety of the story together, in a way that proved that Scotia was a real person and not just a legend. Most of the 'pseudo-histories' of Ireland and Scotland are not taken very seriously, and hence the legend of Scotia has not been taken seriously either.

I wondered to myself - what if one could prove that she really did exist? What if one could prove that Scotia was a real person who left Egypt and was none other than Meritaten, the daughter of renegade Pharaoh Akhenaten? So, I decided that I would dig through all the source material available and the research of others, particularly in Egypt, and see if I could find a trail leading me from Egypt to Spain, Scotland and Ireland. It has been a long time in the making, and an endeavour that I had never expected to find myself engaged in. However, here I am now, some 15 years after I first became interested in Scotia, writing the preface to this book. One might say it is fate, or perhaps just a series of serendipitous occurrences, that led me to be here now writing Scotia's mostly forgotten story. Whatever the case, I feel that it is such a bizarre and intriguing story, that it deserves to be told, for us not to forget who she was, how she ended up in Ireland, and why she left her privileged royal life, in Egypt, behind her.

Scotia, or Scota, as she is sometimes called, has caught the public imagination in recent years, a character from ancient history, famed as the founding matriarch of Scotland, and remembered in myth and legend of both Scotland and Ireland. However, until relatively recently her story, or multiple stories rather, have been regarded as history for millennia, only to be dismissed as fictional from the 19th century onwards.

This can be attributed to the re-evaluation of much of the semi -historical or pseudo-historical tomes of medieval Ireland and Scotland, which have come to be regarded as only very loosely based on historical events or in part, at least, based on pure invention and biblical related fantasy. While there is some truth in this, in that elements of these codices are probably fictitious, modern DNA studies and recent archaeology would tend to lend far more credibility to these ancient accounts than has generally been offered during the 20th and late 19th centuries.

So, what is the truth about Scotia? What is her real story? The answer to that question is a complex one, and one that this book humbly seeks to lay out in front of you, for your consideration. My interest in this character goes back many years, to my first studies of Irish mythology, and indeed more recently, to my two collections of folk takes, about county Kerry. Having had the good fortune to discuss the subject with illustrator Elena Danann, who drew Scotia for 'Kerry Folk Tales', I became fully aware of the Egyptian connection and, in no small way thanks to her input, I was able to piece together the stories of two women, who are one and the same woman – the one who left Egypt and the one who arrived in Ireland, via Scotland.

Her story is obscure and fragmented, hence it has never been told in all its complexity and to its fullest extent, in part, due to the conflation of events and personalities that make building a plausible account of her life that more difficult. By cross-referencing the accounts and archaeology of Egypt with the stories, documents and places of Scotland, and particularly Ireland, a picture of Scotia begins to emerge. This emerging image leads us from Egypt of over 3000 years ago to modern-day Ireland, where a pair of obscure, half-forgotten and difficult to find, graves lie, in the far South-Western corner of the island. I am very fortunate to have visited the site known as Scotia's Grave, on many occasions, leading me to make a previously unrecorded discovery, that may prove crucial to proving the authenticity of the legends. As I mentioned earlier, to this day, the site has never been excavated, and one can only hope that this situation will change in the future and that the two stone arrangements will be explored, to finally discover if they are indeed graves, as described in legend.

I am also most fortunate to have been made aware of the Egyptian connections in relation to Scotia, previously lacking direct knowledge myself of the parallel events, that I believe dovetail with what is recorded in the ancient books of Ireland and Scotland. Perhaps it's pure chance or luck that I should be in the position to bring to light the story of such a nebulous, legendary, royal person. This book has been something of a detective story, uncovering dusty tomes and ancient remains to find the probable or at least plausible, truth of the life of Scotia - one of the most romantically depicted and mysterious heroines in Celtic mythology.

Many people might assume that the ancient sources of Ireland and Scotland, regarding Scotia, are entirely fictional, this is certainly the 'official' view of academia over the last seventy years or more. The referencing of biblical events does nothing to lend credibility to these accounts, but one must consider that this was considered a way of legitimising accounts, in the era that these stories were recorded. However, recent archaeological discoveries, over the last few decades would indicate that some of the well-known biblical events are at least based in real-world events, even if viewed through a very distorted lens.

Likewise, it is possible that the events relating to Scotia are based on real-world events, rather than being entirely fictitious. By tracing the story of Scotia from Egypt, through Spain, Scotland and Ireland I hope to show that her story is not only possible, but quite likely to be based on a half forgotten reality. The real story, as it actually happened, may never be fully revealed, but one can only hope that, with the help of modern archaeological techniques, further light can be thrown into dark corners, illuminating this intriguing mystery.

*

In this book I lay out the case for Scotia's life being that of Meritaten, Egyptian Princess and briefly Queen too. I explore the reasons why she would have fled Egypt, what happened to her afterwards and where she went during the remainder of her life.

To do this I have used the primary sources of Egyptian recorded history, and secondary sources from medieval literature, particularly those of Ireland and Scotland. I also investigated the archaeological finds of Egypt in relation to the Amarna royal family and archaeological finds in Spain, Britain and Ireland, together with recent reports on DNA analysis.

The array of evidence is so substantial that this amazing story is not only quite convincing but highly probable. However, an excavation of Scotia's Grave, in south-west Ireland, is the only way that this story can be proven to be true.

Luke Eastwood, Co. Kerry, Ireland, 2025

THE AMARNA FAMILY TREE

The story of Scotia, who it appears was once known as Meritaten, is a complex one. What happened to her hinges on the difficulties experienced by her father, herself and her siblings, who lived through the Amarna period of Egypt's 18th dynasty.

In order to better understand the complex relationships that are involved, I present this family tree of the main people involved in this story.

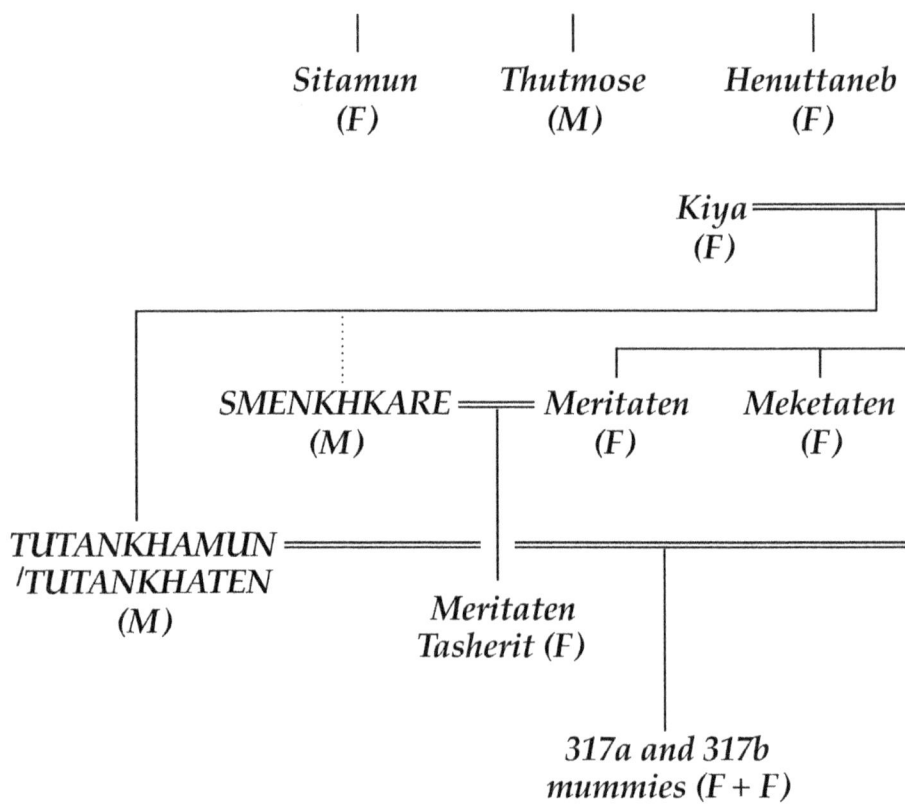

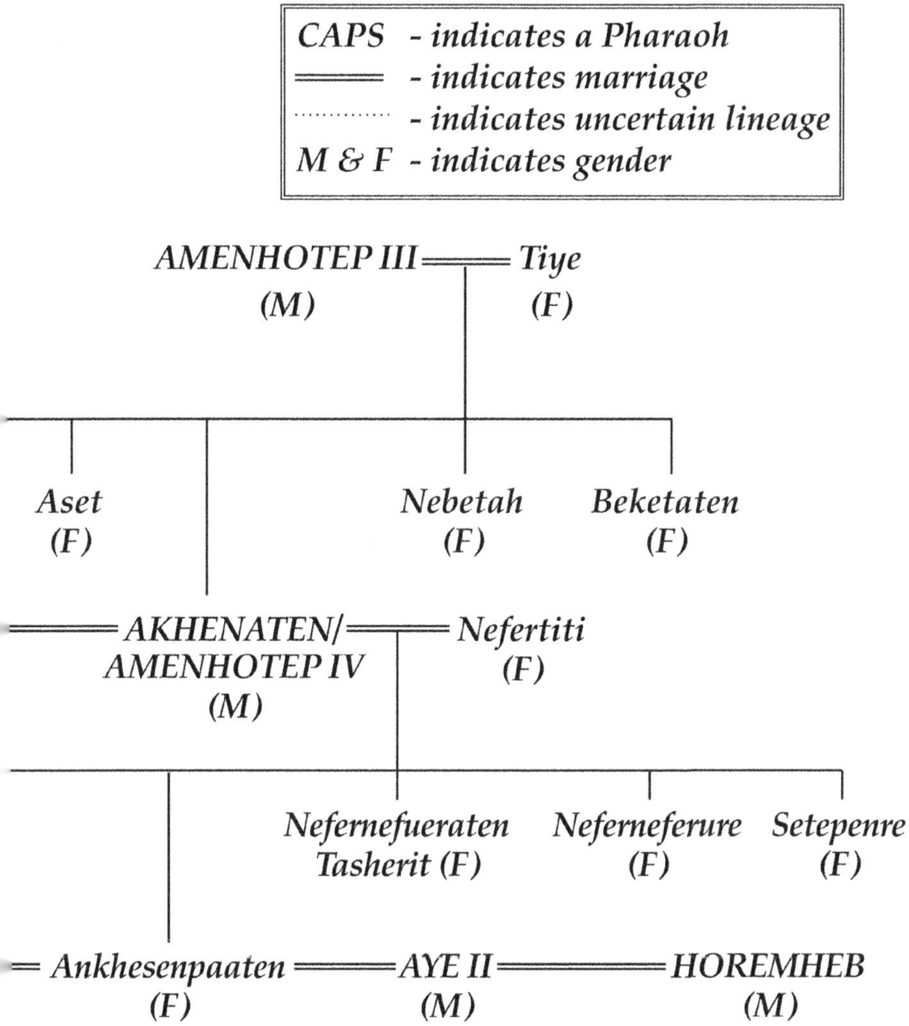

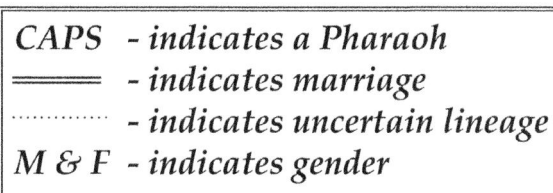

CAPS - indicates a Pharaoh
===== - indicates marriage
.... - indicates uncertain lineage
M & F - indicates gender

AMENHOTEP III===== *Tiye*
(M)   (F)

Aset   *Nebetah* *Beketaten*
(F)   (F)   (F)

===== *AKHENATEN/*===== *Nefertiti*
AMENHOTEP IV   (F)
(M)

Nefernefueraten *Neferneferure* *Setepenre*
Tasherit (F)   (F)   (F)

= *Ankhesenpaaten* ===== *AYE II*===== *HOREMHEB*
(F)   (M)   (M)

NOTE: Ankessenpaaten was married 3 times - to her half-brother Tutankamun, then Aye II, and finally Horemheb. The last Pharaoh she married was not directly related to the Amarna family.

AKHENATEN THE GREAT HERETIC

The story of Scotia begins with her parents in Egypt. It is widely acknowledged that Scotia/Scota is not her given name, or even close to her real name. How she came to be called Scotia or Scota is unknown, but we do know that she was Egyptian. However, there are disputes about who she was to the Egyptians themselves.

Firstly, pinning down the time period she lived in is the initial problem, with some authors and scholars having suggested that she lived around the time of Ramesses II (The Great). Others, such as Mortuary Archaeologist Lorraine Evans, suggested the Amarna period, and more specifically Akhenaten, which I also believe to be correct.

Much of what we know of Scotia comes from Scottish and Irish legend and in particular John of Fordun's 'Chronicle of The Scottish Nation' and Walter Bower's later 'Scotichronicon', a book written in the 15th century, in Scotland. This chronicle of Scottish history consists of 16 books, begun in 1440 and completed in 1447. It spans a vast time period, from the 'pre-history' of myth and the arrival of Scotia up to death of James I of Scotland, in 1437 CE. However, Bower got much of his information from the Greco-Egyptian Manetho, an Egyptian priest and historian, who lived during the early Ptolemaic dynasty, 3rd century BCE. Bower would have read his 'Aegyptiaca' (History of Egypt), which was written in Ancient Greek, and used his kings list (list of pharaohs) for chronology.

In placing Scotia, we must also remember that she left Egypt, which considering her royal position and not being married off to a rival kingdom (she was married within Egypt), would be somewhat unusual. One must wonder why a princess would leave Egypt of her own volition? The most obvious reason, in my opinion, would be some need to leave - such as an obviously dangerous political or military situation, which brings us to the life of her father Akhenaten. As we will see, Akhenaten's reign was very controversial, ending in mysterious circumstances, total reversal of his life's work and eventually the end of his dynasty - reason enough for his eldest daughter to flee perhaps?

The main region of interest is the Eastern Mediterranean and in particular Egypt itself, the Phoenician coast (modern Israel and Lebanon) and southern Iberia (modern Spain), before we arrive eventually at Scotland and Ireland. According

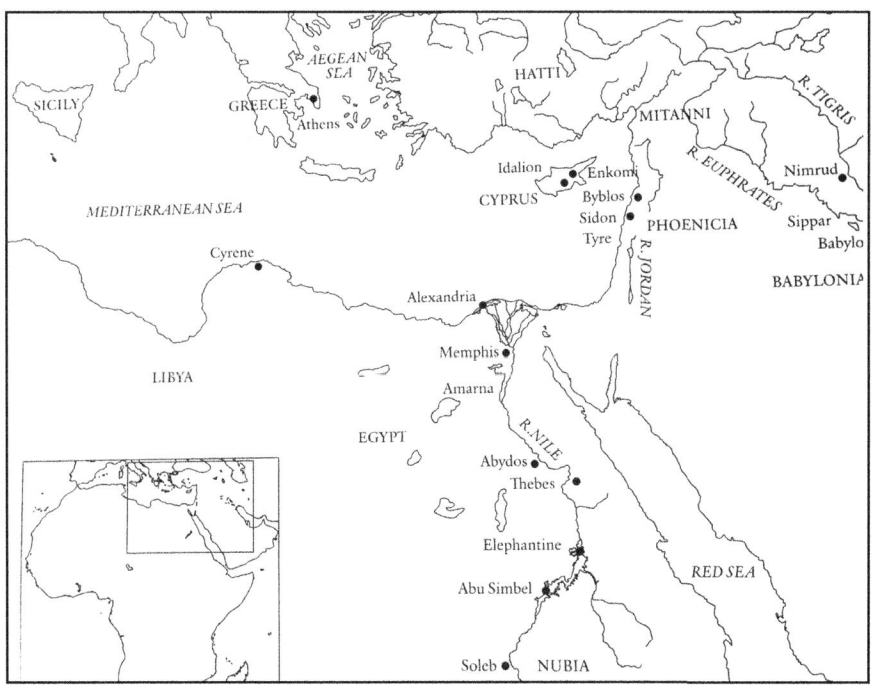

Figure 1: The Eastern Mediterranean. At the time of the 18th Dynasty of Egypt.

to the legends, recounted in the medieval and renaissance literature, Scotia left Egypt with some help (possibly from the Phoenicians or other ancient peoples) and made her way to Spain before leaving the region for Alba/Britannia (Modern Scotland) and Éire/Hibernia (modern Ireland). To give some sense of the geography of some of the main areas of interest, I have included these two maps (figures 1 & 2) - note the position of Amarna, which is the principal focus of events that led to Scotia's flight from Egypt.

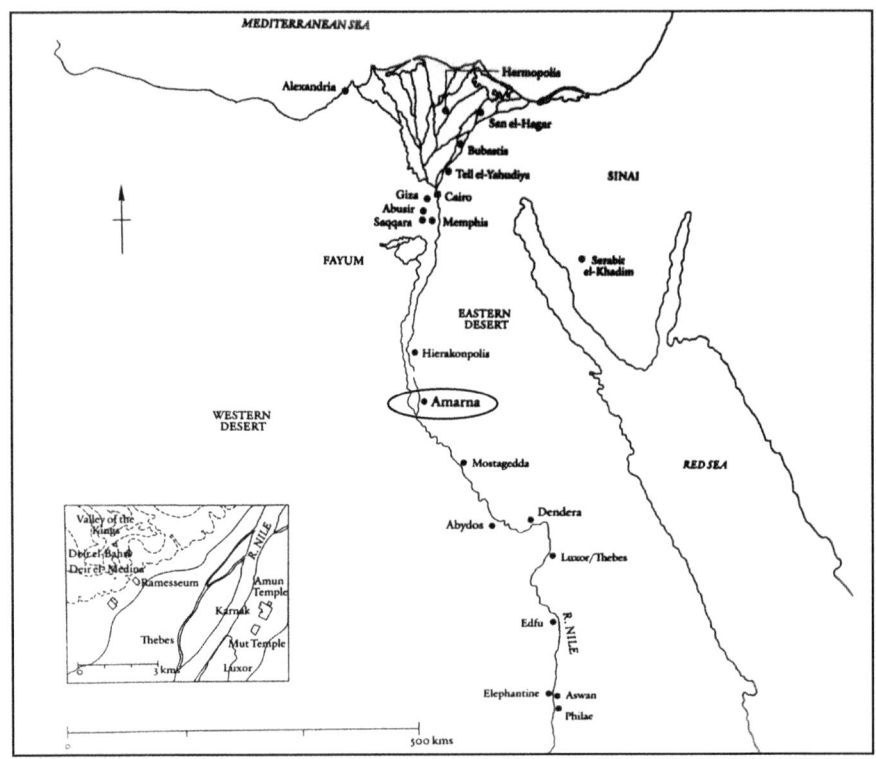

Figure 2: The Nile region. While Memphis was the major centre of power, for a brief period of time Amarna became prominent during the 18th Dynasty.

Amenhotep IV, Pharaoh by Default

Akhenaten famously changed his name. His personal name was Neferkheperure Waenre. Confusing as it is, he was known as Achencheres and he also had an official name on becoming Pharaoh and subsequently changed it a few years after being crowned. At the beginning of his reign he was known as Amenhotep IV (meaning Amun is pleased), reigning (under the two different names) in total from 1353–1336 BCE or possibly 1351–1334 BCE. He was crowned as Amenhotep IV, the second son of Pharaoh Amenhotep III and Amenhotep III's principal wife, named Tiye. The crown prince Thutmoses, Amenhotep III's eldest son and heir, died in the 13th year of his father's reign, leaving Achencheres as next in line, ahead of his sisters: Sitamun, Henuttaneb, Iset, Nebetah, and possibly Beketaten. Egyptian society and Achencheres himself never expected him to succeed his father and become Pharaoh, but child mortality was very common in the ancient world.

As a result of the death of his older brother, Achencheres succeeded his father around 1351/53 BCE as Amenhotep IV, with the expectation that he would continue to reign in the traditional manner that his father had done. What actually happened during his reign could not have been further from what his family, the priesthood and the nation of Egypt expected.

Amenhotep III, a Hard Act to Follow

Amenhotep III is regarded as one of the most successful Pharaohs in Egyptian history, and with 250 or so surviving statues of him, he has the largest number of depictions in existence today. At the point of Amenhotep III's death, he left behind an Egypt at the very height of its power and influence, commanding immense respect from its neighbours and the ancient world in general. His reign was one of tradition and Egypt was a country steeped in age-old political and religious practices, all of which was under the auspices of the powerful priesthood of Amun (Amun-Ra).

Clearly a religious Pharaoh, he commissioned over 700 statues of the goddess Sekhmet, in her lioness features. Sekhmet's name means "who is powerful" and Amenhotep III wished to placate her for the benefit of his own health, the health and prosperity of the nation, assistance in war and to bring about peace. Today around 600 Sekhmet statues have been recovered in Egypt, many of which are in black granite (granodiorite). One cannot say what would have happened had he not been so devoted to Sekhmet, but he obviously felt that gaining her favour contributed to his fairly long life (c. 1400 - 1353 BCE), a successful reign of possibly 38 years and a country that was prosperous and powerful.

It has been suggested that Amenhotep III made his surviving son co-regent but the vast majority of Egyptian scholars dismiss this. However, there is some evidence that Amenhotep IV was co-regent with his father Amenhotep III for at least a year, as indicated by some inscriptions in Luxor, but this is not 100% verified. The official view is that a co-regency never happened or that it was extremely short, which would tend to be supported by Amarna letter EA 27 (a cuneiform tablet) from Amenhotep IV's second year of his reign.

The letter (EA 27) could be seen as a portent, or a sign of things to come for the new Pharaoh. The letter includes a complaint from the king of Mitanni (modern Turkey/Syria border) named Tushratta, claiming that Amenhotep IV had not honoured his father's promise to send him gold statues as part of the marriage arrangement between his daughter Tadukhepa and Amenhotep III. She had become his wife around 1352 BCE, only one year before Amenhotep III died. Tadukhepa had brought with her lavish gifts, such as a gold-plated chariot. For an unknown reason, it appears that Amenhotep IV failed

Figure 3: Painted limestone stela (Circa 1352-1336 BCE) with Pharaoh Amenhotep III and Queen Tiye, the parents of Akenaten (Amenhotep IV), held by the British Museum.

to fulfil the expected reciprocation previously offered by his father only a year or so earlier.

Not long before Amenhotep IV took the throne of Egypt, he married Nefertiti, as his first and principal wife. Little is known of her, but it is speculated that she was his sister and also that she was a foreigner - perhaps Princess Tadukhipa from Mitanni, a Hurdian-speaking state in what is now Northern Syria or perhaps a Scythian royal. Tadukhipa's aunt Gilukhipa (sister of King Tushratta) had married Pharaoh Amenhotep III in his 10th regnal year. Tadukhipa was to marry Amenhotep III more than two decades later (as mentioned previously), not long

Figure 4: Sekhmet statues, commissioned by Akhenaten's father (Amenhotep III), from the British Museum collection.

before he died. So, it is quite likely that Queen Nefertiti and Princess Tadukhipa were one and the same, although there is no definitive proof of this. Nefertiti was his first and primary wife, known as Great Royal Wife and, of her, he is recorded to have said:

"You are not the only one that God created in this world, but you are the only one that God created in my heart."

Contemporary records make it certain that Amenhotep IV had six daughters, most likely with his Great Wife Nefertiti. Among his six daughters, Meritaten was his oldest child, born between regnal year one and five, circa 1356 BCE. The other daughters were Meketaten, Ankhesenpaaten, Nefernefueraten Tasherit, Neferneferure and Setepenre. His son Tutankhaten (later changed to Tutankhamun) was most likely son with his second, minor wife Kiya. There is speculation about Smenkhkare, husband of Meritaten and first successor as Pharaoh, possibly being a son or close relative of Akhenaten/Amenhotep IV, but his origins are unclear.

To begin with, Amenhotep IV ruled in the traditional manner but this all changed around perhaps year three of his reign. Amenhotep IV organised a Sed festival (Feast of the Tail). The festival primarily served to reassert pharaonic authority and state ideology, but in this case it seems to have marked a radical departure from the norm. Some believe that the festival was held to honour the Aten on whose behalf the Pharaoh ruled Egypt. Amenhotep III was considered to have become one with the Aten following his death, and so the Sed festival honoured both the former Pharaoh and the god Aten at the same time. Although of some importance, the Aten paled in significance in comparison with the cult of Amun.

Amun (sometimes called Amen) was long the local tutelary or guardian deity of Thebes, but combined/fused with Ra as Amun-Ra or Amun-Re, the cult became established nationwide around 16th century BCE. The cult of Amun rose to prominence as the Temple of Karnac (at Thebes) became a major religious centre during the early part of the 11th Dynasty. From this point onwards, the cult of Amun and its priesthood was the most powerful religious authority in Egypt. Amun-Ra retained chief importance in the Egyptian pantheon of gods throughout the New Kingdom era, at least until Amenhotep IV reigned. For around 500 years the cult of Amun had held sway, so what Amenhotep IV begun to do was not just unusual; it was revolutionary and to many it was seen as heresy.

It is most likely that the Sed festival was used as a stepping stone to the introduction of the Aten cult and following that the controversial founding of the new capital Akhetaten. It is thought that during the festivities Amenhotep IV only made offerings to the Aten rather than the many gods and goddesses, as was customary which would no doubt have shocked the population and also angered the established hierarchy of Egyptian priesthood.

Not only was Amenhotep IV looking to raise the Aten to a position of prominence, usurping the position held by Amun-Ra, his intention was to obliterate the previously loved and worshipped traditional pantheon of gods. In effect, Amenhotep IV was seeking to create a new monotheistic religion, by elevating one of the Egyptian gods (chosen by himself), whilst practically erasing the remainder of the Egyptian pantheon.

Amenhotep IV Becomes Akhenaten

Two copies of a letter to the Pharaoh from Ipy, the high steward of Memphis are probably the last documents that refer to Akhenaten as Amenhotep IV. These letters, which were found in Gurob/Ghurab (Shedet Oasis 100km South-West of modern Cairo) and informed the Pharaoh that all was well in Memphis, dated to regnal year 5. A boundary stele at Akhetaten (city) dated not much more than a month later had the name Akhenaten carved on it, implying that the Pharaoh changed his name in the intervening period, and thereafter we find no more references to Akhenaten by his original name.

Akhenaten means "Effective for the Aten" and his name change was not purely for effect - he was serious about changing his own religious life, and thereby that of Egypt as a whole. By abandoning Egypt's traditional polytheism he effectively introduced a form of monotheism, based on an existing 'deity', the Aten. Introducing Atenism, a religion that worshipped and was entirely centred around the Aten, was a radical departure from Egypt's past, that had always been polytheistic.

The Aten existed since the Old Kingdom. as a noun meaning "disc". The sun was called the "disc of the day" where Ra was thought to reside, the sun itself was not worshipped, a common misbelief, but the divine power of the creation/universe, symbolised by the sun disc. The Aten was the disc of the sun and was originally an aspect of the preeminent creator god (originally unisex) Ra, the sun god in traditional ancient Egyptian religion.

While the Aten was worshiped in previous eras, and more so under the reign of Akhenaten's father, Amenhotep III, it was made the sole deity of the Egyptian state and the official cult or religion of Egypt by Akhenaten.

The first known reference to Aten the sun-disc as a deity is in 'The Story of Sinuhe', a text that dates to the reign of Amenemhat III in the 12th dynasty, around 1800 BCE, in which the deceased king is described as rising as a god to the heavens and "uniting with the sun-disc, the divine body merging with its maker".

Founding A new Capital

As soon as Akhenaten had decided to change his name he founded a new capital on the banks of the Nile about half way between the historical capital (Thebes) and Memphis. This new city was called Akhetaten after himself and was to become not just the home of the royal family but the centre of his new monotheistic religion. Other important sites where the religion was prominently established were the old capital of Thebes and Heliopolis (City of the Sun), North-East of modern Cairo. Akhenaten, no doubt to the consternation of the long-established Egyptian priesthood of the old gods (particularly Amun and Amun-Ra) closed down all of the old temples, permitting only the worship of the royal family and the Aten itself.

The new capital city was a place of worship of the Aten, with Akhenaten formally dedicating the city to the god and emphasising the royal residences' efforts (on behalf of Egypt) in worship. All of the major principles of the Aten cult were recorded via inscriptions on temples and tombs from the period, although much of the inscriptions have been damaged

Figure 5: Akhenaten in a blue crown, holding an offering plate, circa 1372 BCE (held by Museum of Egyptian Antiquities, Cairo. Photograph by Helena Zacharias).

or destroyed in the aftermath of the Amarna period.

Akhenaten's new dogma diverged significantly from the tradition of ancient Egyptian polytheism and the typical custom of temples being hidden and more enclosed the further one went into the site. In contrast, the temples of the Aten were open, with no roofs, in order to allow the rays of the sun inside. No statues of the Aten were allowed as they were seen as idolatry, and the Aten did not have a humanoid form anyway. Instead, the humanoid gods of the old pantheon were replaced by Stella (wall carvings) or statues with highly stylised (non-traditional) representations of Akhenaten or of Akhenaten and his family venerating the Aten and receiving

Figure 6: Gold finger ring baring the name Akhenaten, circa 1352-1336 BCE. Accompanying his name is the inscription "all Egypt is in adoration", a statement that would later prove to be entirely untrue (held by the British Museum). .

the Ankh (the breath of life), from the Aten. In comparison to periods before and after the Amarna period, the priesthood had little to do since offerings, such as fruits, flowers and cakes, were limited and the traditional oracles were not needed or permitted.

In the new religion of the Aten, the daily service of purification, anointment and clothing of the divine image, that was traditionally found in ancient Egyptian religion, was no longer performed. Instead of this, incense and food-stuff offerings such as meats, wines, and fruits were placed onto open-air altars (the temples were roofless). Akhenaten giving offering to Aten has him consecrating the sacrificed goods with a royal sceptre in many carved depictions. Also, instead of the traditional-processions utilising a barque (religiously significant boat), the royal family rode in a chariot on festival days. One can imagine that all these changes were a shock to the Egyptian people and no-doubt a great annoyance to the conservative Egyptian priesthood, particularly those of Amun-Ra.

Akhenaten also moved his entire government to the new city (also referred to as Amarna, El-Amarna, or Tell el-Amarna). In Atenism, the day time was sacred and the time to be productive and creative - night was seen as a time to fear, due to the absence of the sun, leaving the world in darkness. Work was done best when the sun, and thereby also the Aten, was present. According to Akhenaten's new mythology the Aten created all countries of the world and the world's people, and cared for every living creature. According to the inscriptions, the Aten created the River Nile in the sky (rain) for the Syrians, one can assume the actual Nile was an earthly reflection of this cosmic river.

In the new dogma the divine rays of the sun disk only held out life and blessings to Akhenaten and his royal family. This made Akhenaten the sole representative (with the exception of his blood family) and because of this, non-royals could not receive from the Aten directly but instead received life from Akhenaten and his Queen Nefertiti. However, this was

Figure 7: Limestone stela of Akhenaton and Nefertiti seated, holding 3 of their daughters, under the rays of the sun god Aton giving Ankh-symbols to them. Amarna-period, ca. 1350-1340 BCE (held by Berlin Neues Museum. Public domain photograph).

only in exchange for loyalty to them and to the Aten. In inscriptions, like the Hymn to the Aten and the King, the Aten is depicted as caring for the people through Akhenaten, placing the royal family as intermediaries for the worship of the Aten. This was revolutionary and dispensed with the need for an extensive network of priesthood for the administering of rites and festivals in service to the old gods. According to this new theology, all the people of Egypt needed was their god-Pharaoh, priest-Pharaoh Akhenaten (and his family) who would provide the divine sustenance of the Aten to the people directly via themselves!

Of course, being Pharaoh, the priesthood could not protest or openly do anything about this, or show any signs of opposition. However, one can be assured that in creating his own off-shoot religion, Akhenaten made an enemy of the Egyptian priesthood (particularly the priests of Amun-Ra) and possibly many within his government, the military and throughout Egyptian society as a whole. Although everyone would have paid lip-service to Akhenaten and his new dogma, archaeological evidence suggests the closing of the state temples of other Egyptian gods probably did not stop household worship of the traditional pantheon. Perhaps the people continued to worship the old gods in secret? Perhaps away from Amarna, Thebes and Heliopolis the priesthood and the people would have quietly carried on their traditional practices, but most likely in private, rather than in public?

A Short-lived Cult

Akhenaten has probably envisaged his capital city and his new cult lasting for a thousand years or more, but alas it was not to be. The reign of Amenhotep IV was not exceptional, but when he became Akhenaten, things took a turn for the worse, and this did not improve during the course of his reign.

One can only the imagine the huge cost of building a new capital city, the cost of new temples around Egypt and the cost of implementing the new religion. It would appear that the location of Amarna was based on the revelation "the Aten alone brought him to the spot". Perhaps the fact that Amarna lies in a gap in precipitous cliffs, allowing the rising sun to be seen is the key factor here. This would fit with Akhenaten's obsession with the sun, as a symbol of the power of the Aten. The eastern bank was not very fertile, unlike the western bank and so made a suitable spot to build a city, with stone from the surrounding hills, not very far from the Nile itself. However it was not convenient in terms of provision of food, with no arable land or pasture near by. Although

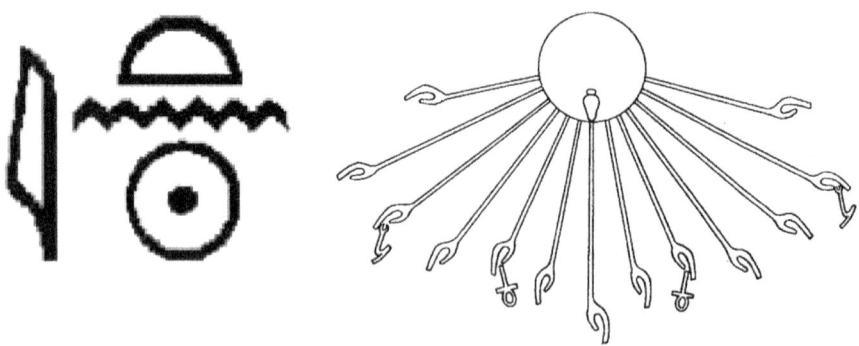

Figure 8: The Aten hieroglyph. (pronounced ee-ten, includes the four symbols for reed, bread, water and sun, but they have no significance themselves).

Figure 9: The Aten symbol/pictogram, showing the divine rays of the sun emanating from it.

thriving Hermopolis was fairly close by there is little else to recommend a site so far away from the rest of Egypt's cities and far from its borders.

During the course of his reign, Akhenaten was preoccupied with religious matters and so one could say that he neglected his duties as Pharaoh, head of state, commander of the armies and his responsibilities for the financial and imperial interests of Egypt. It would seem that he was primarily interested in the cult of the Aten and the building and establishment of his capital Akhetaten at Amarna.

In the tomb of Aye II, is 'The Hymn to the Aten' inscribed in hieroglyths on one of the walls. In Akhenaten's reign Aye became Overseer of All the Horses of His Majesty, the highest rank in the elite charioteering division of the army, and also Fan-bearer on the Right Side of the King, Acting Scribe of the King, beloved by him, and God's Father. Hence due to his important position he was permitted to build a tomb for himself (Southern Tomb 25) at Amarna. There are several copies of 'The Hymn to the Aten' but many of them have been damaged or partially destroyed. The copy found in Aye II's tomb is complete, presumably only because Aye II was not buried there, but at tomb WV23 at The Valley of the Kings, near Luxor and his original tomb was forgotten.

"The Hym to the Aten

Worship (Re-Horakhty who Rejoices in the Horizon) (In his Name as the Shu who is in the Aten) living forever and ever, the Living Aten, the Great One who is in Jubilee, Master of all that the Aten encircles, Master of Heaven, Master of the Earth, Master of the Per-

Aten inAkhet-Aten; and the King of Upper and Lower Egypt, the one Living on Maat, Master of Regalia (Akhenaten), the long lived; and the Foremost Wife of the King, whom he loves, the Mistress of Two Lands (Nefer-nefru-Aten Nefertiti), living, well, and young forever and ever.

He says:

You rise in perfection on the living Aten, who started life. horizon of the sky, Whenever you are risen upon the eastern horizon you fill every land with your perfection. You are appealing, great, sparkling, high over every land; your rays hold together the lands as have made. far as everything you have made.

Since you are Re, you reach as far as they do, and you curb them for your beloved son. Although you are far away, your rays are upon the land; you are in their faces, yet your departure is not observed. Whenever you set on the western horizon, the land is in darkness in the manner of death.They sleep in a bedroom with heads under the covers, and one eye does not see another. If all their possessions which are under their heads were stolen, they would not know it.

Every lion who comes out of his cave and all the serpents bite, for darkness is a blanket. The land is silent now, because he who made them is at rest on his horizon. But when day breaks you are risen upon the horizon, and you shine as the Aten in the daytime. When you dispel darkness and you give forth your rays the two lands are in festival, alert and standing on their feet, now that you have raised them up.

Their bodies are clean, / and their clothes have been put on; their arms are ‹lifted› in praise at your rising. The entire land performs its work: all the cattle are content with their fodder, trees and plants grow, birds fly up to their nests, their wings ‹extended› in praise for your Ka. All the kine prance on their feet; everything which flies up and alights, they live when you have risen for them. The barges sail upstream and downstream too, for every way IS open at your rising. The fishes in the river leap before your face when your rays are in the sea.

You who have placed seed in woman and have made sperm into man, who feeds the son in the womb of his mother, who quiets him with something to stop his crying; you are the nurse in the womb, giving breath to nourish all that has been begotten. When he comes down from the womb to breathe on the day he is born, you open up his mouth completely', and supply his needs. When the fledgling in the egg speaks in the shell, you give him air inside it to sustain him. When you grant him his allotted time to break out from the egg, he comes out from the egg to cry out at his fulfilment, and he goes upon his legs when he has come forth from it.

How plentiful it is, what you have made, although they are hidden from view, sole god, without another beside you; you created the earth when as you wished, you were by yourself, ‹before» mankind, all cattle and kine, all beings on land, who fare upon their feet, and all beings in the air, who fly with their wings.

The lands of Khor and Kush and the land of Egypt: you have set every man in his place, you have allotted their needs, every one of them according to his diet, and his lifetime is counted out. Tongues are separate in speech, and their characters / as well; their skins are different, for you have differentiated the foreigners. In the underworld you have made a Nile that you may bring it forth as you wish to feed the populace, since you made them for yourself, their utter master, growing weary on their account, lord of every land. For them the Aten of the daytime arises, great in awesomeness.

All distant lands, you have made them live, for you have set a Nile in the sky that it may descend for them and make waves upon the mountains like the sea to irrigate the fields in their towns. How efficient are your designs, Lord of eternity: a Nile in the sky for the foreigners and all creatures that go upon their feet, a Nile coming back from the underworld for Egypt.

Your rays give suck to every field: when you rise they live, and they grow for you. You have made the seasons to bring into being all you have made: the Winter to cool them, the Heat that you may be felt. You have made a far-off heaven in which to rise in order to observe everything you have made. Yet you are alone, rising in your manifestations as the Living Aten: appearing, glistening, being afar, coming close; you make millions of transformations of yourself. Towns, harbours, fields, roadways, waterways: every eye beholds you upon them, for you are the Aten of the daytime on the face of the earth. When you go forth every eye [is upon you]. You have created their sight but not to see (only) the body which you have made.

You are my desire, and there is no other who knows you except for your son (Nefer-kheperu-Re Wa-en-Re),' for you have apprised him of your designs and your power. The earth came forth into existence by your hand, and you made it. When you rise, they live; when you set, they die. You are a lifespan in yourself; one lives by you.

Eyes are upon your perfection until you set: all work is put down when you rest in the west. When (you) rise, (everything) grows for the King and (for) everyone who hastens on foot, because you have founded the land and you have raised them for your son who has come forth from your body, the King of Upper and Lower Maat, Egypt, the one Living on Lord of the Two Lands (Nefer-kheperu-Re

Wa-en-Re), son of Re, the one Living on Maat, Master of Regalia, (Akhenaten), the long lived, and the Foremost Wife of the King, whom he loves, the Mistress of the Two Lands, (Nefer-nefru-Aten Nefertiti), living and young, forever and ever.

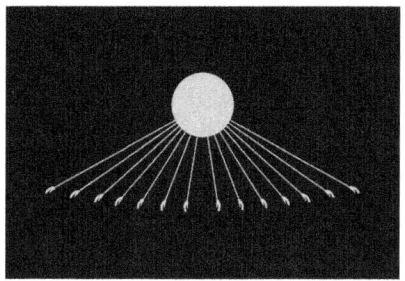

Figure 10: Hieroglyths on an internal wall of the original (unused) tomb of Aye II (Amarna, Egypt. Photograph by Helena Zacharias).

International matters, such as dealing with rival empires, securing the borders and unruly possessions, ensuring a good food supply and other resources don't appear to have been made a priority by Akhenaten, perhaps in his religious zeal, he believed that the Aten would ensure prosperity for Egypt, without him paying full attention to the usual duties expected of a Pharaoh.

The best source of information available on Akhenaten's international relations is the Amarna Letters, which is a cache of 382 diplomatic texts and literary and educational materials mostly discovered in 1887, with additional material found up until as late as 1979. The diplomatic correspondence comprises of tablets (of clay) written in the Sumerian cuneiform script (in Akkadian language), which was common for international relations at the time in the East. The trove contains correspondence of Amenhotep III, Akhenaten, and Tutankhamun with rulers of the vassal states, various subjects through Egyptian military outposts and the foreign rulers of Mitanni, the Hittite Kingdom. Babylonia, Assyria, Syria, Canaan, Alashiya and Arzawa. The letters date from c. 1360 – 1332 BCE. Egyptian rulers prior to Akhenaten had dealt with military threats to the Egyptian empire, particularly under Thutmose III, but this process began to reverse under Amenhotep III, who used marriages to secure peace with neighbouring kingdoms. This proved successful for Amenhotep III and his reign is generally regarded as a successful one, during which Egypt increased its prestige. Under his son Akhenaten political and international relations were somewhat neglected. This neglect had serious effects and the stability of the empire began to come under serious threat, particularly from the Hittites, who in particular threatened the kingdom of Mitanni.

An Amarna letter details a complaint by Tushratta (King of Mitanni and relative of Queen Nefertiti) to Akhenaten about the situation:

"I...asked your father Mimmureya [i.e., Amenhotep III] for statues of solid cast gold, ... and your father said, 'Don't talk of giving statues just of solid cast gold. I will give you ones made also of lapis lazuli. I will give you too, along with the statues, much additional gold and [other] goods beyond measure.' Every one of my messengers that were staying in Egypt saw the gold for the statues with their own eyes. ... But my brother [i.e., Akhenaten] has not sent the solid

[gold] statues that your father was going to send. You have sent plated ones of wood. Nor have you sent me the goods that your father was going to send me, but you have reduced [them] greatly. Yet there is nothing I know of in which I have failed my brother. ... May my brother send me much gold. ... In my brother's country gold is as plentiful as dust. May my brother cause me no distress. May he send me much gold in order that my brother [with the gold and m]any [good]s may honour me."

Another prime example of the dissatisfaction of foreign rulers with Akhenaten's regime can be found in a letter from Burna-Buriash, the king of Babylon. The long tradition of exchanging gifts between kingdoms and/or empires helped maintain good relations and the letter clearly indicates Akhenaten's neglect of this duty through inadequate gifts. Burna-Buriash's letter complains of the poor quality and quantity of gifts in comparison to those that he had sent to Akhenaten. Clearly the Babylonian king felt sufficiently insulted or annoyed to write in complaint. One can only guess how such a situation developed.

Was Akhenaten so wrapped up in his new city and new religion that he failed to pay attention to such matters? Did he appoint incompetent or corrupt officials to handle the process of gift exchanges? If the Pharaoh was totally distracted it is quite possible that officials acting on his behalf embezzled funds, stole or sold off items that should have been allocated for gift giving. One might also speculate that the vast sums of money spent on the new city of Amarna, new temples across the country and neglect of trade alliances may have led the royal coffers to become depleted, perhaps leading to a 'cheapskate' approach to the exchange of gifts with foreign rulers. Whatever the case may be, we can be certain that rulers of nearby kingdoms were not impressed with Akhenaten's behaviour, which of course led to a worsening of Egypt's international relations with its neighbours.

Figure 11: Letter in the Amarna Royal Archives from Burna-Buriash on the exchange of gifts, circa 1352-1336 BCE (held by the British Museum).

Egypt's allies fighting against the Hittite empire implored Akhenaten for help, mostly in the form of troops but he ignored their pleas. The northern frontier difficulties provoked further trouble in Canaan and again, instead of sending troops to help, Akhenaten refused to intervene and help Rib-Hadda, the king of Byblos. The events I have described are just a few examples of Akhenaten's inaction and neglect of his duties as Pharaoh.

The tradition of triumphal promenades through Egyptian dominions and allied lands by the Pharaoh was a morale booster that declined under Amenhotep III and was abandoned by Akhenaten, who preferred to sit in state at Amarna, lavishing money on the city and spectaculars there, for the inhabitants and visiting foreign dignitaries. As regards the army - abuse and corruption increased during his reign and there is no evidence that Akhenaten ever took the field in war, like many of his predecessors (and successors) would have done.

To make matters worse, there were a number of notable deaths amongst the royal family of Amarna. Firstly, Akhenaten's second Queen, Kiya, died in the 9th year of his reign, much loved and mourned according to inscriptions. Sufficient of her funeral goods have survived into modern times to indicate that she was granted a lavish funeral, with no expense spared. It is widely believed that she is the mother of Tutankhaten (later Tutenkhamun), indicated by grave goods belonging to her that were found in his tomb.

The death of Queen Tiye (Akhenaten's mother), and not long after, that of Akhenaten and Nefertiti's second daughter Meketaten would have been a huge blow. Both presumably were buried in the royal wadi east of Amarna city (Akhetaten) itself

Figure 12: Close-up of an alabaster canopic jar featuring a bust of Queen Kiya, 2nd wife of Akhenaten. This item was found in the tomb of TutenKhamun (held by Museum of Egyptian Antiquities, Cairo. Photograph by Helena Zacharias).

- the tombs of the royal family were prepared well in advance, presumably at the same time as the city itself was being constructed. It was a common practice to prepare the tombs of the Pharaoh and his family members during the reign, often beginning immediately after it commenced. Construction was a lengthy process and with the uncertainty of how long people would live (life expectancy was much shorter than today) it was considered wise to prepare tombs well in advance of when they might be needed.

At the end of Akhenaten's reign there seems to be a great deal of confusion, with contradictory versions of events. There appears to be alternate versions of the succession after Akhenaten, up until the point that Tutankhaten became Pharaoh. The identities of Smenkhare and Neferneferuaten are disputed, with candidates given as Nefertiti, Meritaten, Ankhesenpaaten and Tutankhaten, depending on whose theory one adheres to.

In the ancient Egyptian king lists Akhenaten and his progeny were completely erased - thus the 18th dynasty jumps from Amenhotep III directly to Tutankhamun. It appears that this was the work of Horemheb, the final Pharaoh of the 18th dynasty. The 18th dynasty section of the king list given today is somewhat different from that from the 19th dynasty onwards.

Ancient Egyptian king list:
Amenhotep III
Tutankhamun
Aye II
Horemheb

Modern Egyptian king list:

Amenhotep III
Amenhotep IV (later changed to Akhenaten)
Smenkhare
Neferneferuaten (disputed)
Tutankhaten (later changed to Tutankhamun)
Aye II
Horemheb

Around year 14 of Akhenaten's reign Nefertiti appears to have also died, no record of her exists after that date. Although nothing has been found at Amarna, she was presumably buried at the royal wadi, along with other members of the royal family. However, there is some controversy over what happened to Nefertiti. She is perhaps the most famous of Egyptian queens, possibly with the exception of Cleopatra. Cleopatra was a descendent of the Greek Ptolemy I Soter, and like her, Nefertiti was almost definitely also of foreign descent. While some dispute her foreign birth, the fact that there are no records of her existence in Egypt, prior to her marriage to Amenhotep IV, is indicative that that she came from elsewhere.

Some scholars believe that Nefertiti ruled briefly as a female Pharaoh (After the death of her husband Akhenaten) known by the throne name Neferneferuaten. This would have been immediately before the ascension of Tutankhaten (later Tutankhamun) although this theory is hotly debated and generally disregarded by mainstream Egyptologists. Given that she is definitely recorded as dying during the reign of Akhenaten, it is hard to believe that she reigned after his death.

Perhaps a year after the death of Nefertiti, Smenkhkare was crowned as Akhenaten's co-regent on his reaching the age of manhood. He was also married to Akhenaten's eldest daughter

Figure 13: Bust of Queen Tiye, wife of Amenhotep III and mother of Akhenaten, who died in 1338 BCE (held by Altes Museum Berlin.Photograph by Helena Zacharias).

Meritaten, thereby giving legitimacy to his future rule as Pharaoh and any children that they might have together. This marriage was a way of securing the royal line, given that Akhenaten's only living son Tutankhaten, was still only a young boy.

Meritaten, known to her family affectionately as Mayati, is mentioned in some correspondence between Akhenaten and the rulers of Babylon and Tyre, although author Ralph Ellis is of the opinion that it is his younger daughter, Ankhesenpaaten, who is the one referred to, and that she was the one who would go on to be referred to in Ireland and Scotland as Scotia/ Scota. Personally, I think there is convincing evidence that it was Meritaten who left Egypt, but I shall come to that in due course. In fact Ankhesenpaaten/Ankhesenamun was married three times to three different Pharaohs - Tutankhaten, Aye and Horemheb. Ankhesenpaaten outlasted everyone else in the 18th dynasty. Her final husband (Horemheb) was the last Pharaoh of this dynasty as they had no children together.

It would appear that following the death of his chief Queen Nefertiti, Akhenaten decided to elevate his daughter Meritaten to the position of consort and also the 'mistress of his house', perhaps because he had already lost his second, although minor, wife. This decision would have been about securing the succession and the continuation of the Aten cult within Egypt, via his direct descendants.

It seems that shortly after this decision was made, the sunshades and temples dedicated to Kiya, and possibly also for Nefertiti were altered - adapted for the new Queen in waiting and heiress, Meritaten. On becoming co-regent Smenkhkare's new wife, Meritaten, automatically became Queen of Egypt. With all these

Figure 14: Bust of Nefertiti, 1st wife of Akhenaten and mother of his 6 daughters (from the Egyptian Museum of Berlin collection. Photograph by Philip Pikart).

personal losses, the troubles with the Hittites and Canaan, internal strife over the unpopular Aten cult, draining of the royal treasuries and disgruntled army and priesthood, the final years of Akhenaten's reign must have been uncomfortable, to say the least.

A Strange Death

Amid a kingdom full of difficulties and tragic deaths, Akhenaten suddenly died himself, in circumstances that are more or less unknown. Author Cyril Aldred suggest that Akhenaten died after the grape harvest in the 17th year of his reign. Immediately after this, possibly Neferneferuaten was Pharaoh, but also possibly there is some confusion with Smenkhkare who is known to have been crowned as the new Pharaoh, ruling alongside Meritaten, the daughter of Akhenaten. There is also the confusion of Neferneferuaten with Nefertiti, his primary Queen, who was already deceased.

There has been much speculation about what actually happened to Akhenaten, including suggestions that he was murdered by someone in a high position - perhaps a general of the army or a High-Priest of Amun? We do not know, it is all really a matter of guesswork. What is strange is that there is nothing to go on historically, only conjecture, probably because many of the records of this period were destroyed by Horemheb and his descendants in the 19th dynasty. What we do know is that the royal tombs at Amarna, prepared for Akhenaten and his family, were empty and largely unused. It would appear that he was either never buried there or that his body and accoutrements were moved to another location, away from his capital city at Amarna (Akhetaten).

The Amarna tomb of Akhenaten was discovered by locals around 1887-88 CE. The tomb had been violently destroyed after the death of the Pharaoh and some of the reliefs were damaged, although many of them survived undamaged or only slightly damaged. One of the chambers was perhaps dedicated to his mother, Queen Tiye, another perhaps to his daughter Meketaten.

The funerary equipment discovered inside the tomb was very massively damaged and fragmentary, a clear sign of looting or vandalism. During their explorations researchers found the red granite sarcophagus of Akhenaten, a model boat (barque made of wood), fragments of storage vessels, ostraca, jewellery, a canopic chest, fragments of furniture, a lion bier, a sculptor's model, a throw-stick, a limestone stele, uraeus heads, inlays, a knife and pieces of textile. Considering the destruction, quite a lot of material was left behind, which may indicate deliberate destruction rather than the remains of a grave robbery. The researchers also found some bones – which have not been identified as yet.

What is clear is that the decorations of the tomb were destroyed after Akhenaten's death, but with little care and attention. Maybe this was done in a hurried and unsystematic way, as some of the depictions of the royal family survived, which are now famous the world over. All of the reliefs in this tomb are in the characteristic style of Akhenaten's unique art, which is notably different from the traditional Egyptian art from both earlier and later periods.

What is now known as Tomb WV25 is an unfinished tomb in the West Valley of the Valley of the Kings, at Thebes. It is the unfinished remains of a royal tomb, which was undecorated, and incomplete and generally thought to be the abandoned tomb of Akhenaten. It was discovered by Italian archaeologist Giovanni Battista Belzoni in 1817. Belzoni also discovered 8 mummies from the 3rd intermediate period inside the unfinished

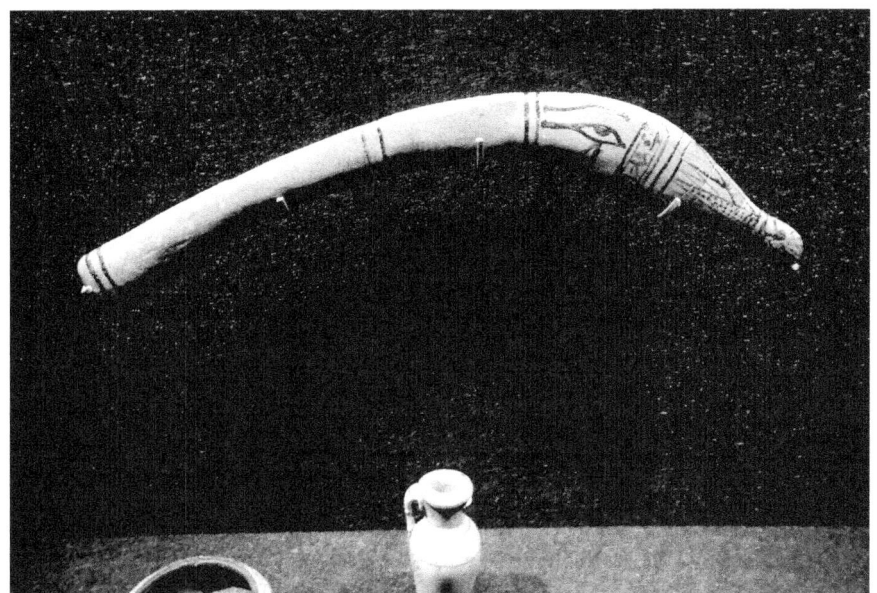

Figure 15: Faience Throwstick (glazed ceramic decorated with wedjat-eye amulets) belonging to Pharaoh Akhenaten. Typically tomb scenes show hunting with weapons such as a this, but this item would have been too fragile, purely symbolic and intended for magical use (held by the British Museum).

tomb. The tomb was excavated again in 1972 by the Egyptian Expedition of the University of Minnesota (UMEE), which was led by Otto Schaden, but in 1817 Belzoni noted:

"We immediately entered, and found ourselves on a staircase eight feet wide and ten feet high, at the bottom of which were four mummies in their cases, lying flat on the ground with their heads towards the outside. Farther on were four more, lying in the same direction."

He also observed that the mummies were similar in their painted and varnished cases, although one was covered in a pall. One was wrapped in finer quality linen and garlands of leaves and flowers; it appeared to have been re-wrapped as, upon investigation, all that remained of the mummy was yellow-coloured bones. Two large metal plates, one with wedjat (Eye of Horus) eyes, and the other in the shape of a winged disc were found in the wrappings.

It would appear that the eight mummies had originally been held somewhere else and had been deposited here for safe-keeping, perhaps only on a temporary basis? If that was the case then they were never retrieved and remained in situ for over three thousand years.

In the later re-excavation of 1972 large amounts of late 18th dynasty pottery were discovered. A single foundation pit, which was empty, was later found on the eastern side of the entrance in 2001 by Richard Wilkinson. He later suggested that the deposit may have been originally discovered by Belzoni and emptied by him.

Excavation in the interior of the tomb found the stairway contained rock and fill; portions of the upper stairs, mummy wrappings and fragments were also discovered. It would appear that this tomb was filled in, in part by destroying the upper parts of the stair case, presumably to conceal the existence of the tomb and its contents. Currently we do not know who the occupants of the tomb were, is it possible that this is the resting place of many of the Amarna royal family? Seeing as the graves of Akhenaten's family in Amarna were empty, or in some cases never used, it is quite possible that these eight bodies are the remains of Akhenaten's family.

It is quite likely that the tomb was originally intended for Amenhotep IV (later Akhenaten) and remained unfinished simply because Akhenaten had wished himself and his entire family to be buried at his new capital city at Amarna. This would make perfect sense as no Pharaoh would see the logic of completing two tombs for himself, one of which would never be used. If the intended tomb at Amarna was abandoned in a hurry, which appears to be the case, perhaps the remains of the royal family were moved to here?

Those loyal to Akhenaten and to the cult of the Aten would have been well aware of the desire for change from the priesthood of Amun, politicians, generals and other people of importance. Once Akhenaten's dynasty was crumbling, they would have known that not only the royal city, but the royal graves too, would have been under threat. It seems to me to be highly probable that loyal servants of the Amarna royalty removed the bodies of Akhenaten and his family, and relocated them to a safer, probably secret place. This may well have happened in a hurry, perhaps in panic, with plans to re-inter them properly - a plan that never was completed.

Another burial site of great interest is KV55, a tomb also in the Valley of the Kings, Thebes. It was discovered in 1907 by Edward R. Ayrton while working for Theodore M. Davis (a wealthy private sponsor for the Egyptian Antiquities Service). For many years it has been speculated that the body found in this tomb was that of Akhenaten, but this could not be confirmed. However, the results of genetic and other scientific tests, published in February 2010, confirmed that the person buried there was both the son of Amenhotep III and the father of Tutankhamun, i.e. he was Amenhotep IV/Akhenaten.

In addition to establishing the identity of the mummy, the study found that the age of the man, at the time of his death was consistent with that of Akhenaten, giving us almost 100% certainty that it is indeed Akhenaten's body.

The identification of KV55's single occupant has been problematic: it is presumed to be a royal cache and reburial dating from the late 18th dynasty, prepared after the abandonment of Amarna and the ransacking of Akhenaten's tomb there. It is located a few meters to the west of the tomb of Ramesses IX (KV6). Based on the artefacts recovered, it is also possible that the burial once contained more than one occupant, either interred on one occasion or over a period of time. Queen Tiye (Akhenaten's mother) is most often named as another potential occupant of the tomb.

The tomb was clearly looted and damaged in ancient times, but it still contained treasures which overwhelmed the researchers who found it. The list of findings is impressive. According to the original inventory, it contained: bier fragments (gold), a vulture collar (gold), a floral collar (gold – inlaid), pall rosettes (gold, bronze), a goose head (silver), a shrine and shrine fittings (wood, gilded, and bronze), coffin and coffin fittings, uraeus from the statue, statue socle (wood), bes figures, earring fasteners, necklace ornaments, plaques, amulets, beads, foil fragments, canopic jars (calcite), boxes and furniture fragments, a wooden hieratic label, tools and fragments of tools, bricks, knives, boomerangs (throwsticks), grapes, papyrus rolls, boxes, pebbles, some small ritual items, and an ostracon (potshard or limestone flake used for writing on) with a plan drawn on it.

Some of the items found belonged to Akhenaten's second wife Kiya, or to his father Amenhotep III, and his mother Tiye. One of the clay seals contains the name of his son Tutankhaten. Most

Figure 16: Sarcophagus KV55, believed to be that of Akhenaten due to the vandalism of the coffin. Note that the golden funeral mask has been almost completely torn off (held by Museum of Egyptian Antiquities, Cairo. Photograph by Hans Ollermann).

important of all was the skeleton of a very badly mummified man. The body lay in the coffin under a representation of a Pharaoh without a face i.e. the golden face mask had been forcibly removed. This suggests that the priesthood of Amun or some other opponent(s) of the Pharaoh punished Akhenaten by erasing his face from the coffin. It is thought that, in the ancient Egyptian belief system, a person whose portraits and inscriptions of their name were destroyed lived an eternal life without knowing their identity. To do such a thing to a Pharaoh's coffin would be the ultimate insult.

After years of debate, ended only by genetic testing, most researchers agree that the remains belong to Pharaoh Akhenaten. According to DNA tests, the man discovered in KV55 was definitely the father of Tutankhaten/Tutenkhamun.

Investigations showed that the tomb was re-entered at a later time, almost certainly during the 20th dynasty, but it may well have been robbed earlier too. At some point, it is possible that other occupants of the tomb (if there were any) were removed and relocated to KV35 or WV25. It also appears that some of the artefacts were desecrated as was the remaining mummy. While it cannot be proven beyond doubt that another body or several other bodies had been stored here at KV55, it seems quite likely given the controversy and hatred surrounding the entire Amarna dynasty that existed at the time. Undoubtedly there would have been the need to rescue any bodies from their tombs at Amarna and not only to relocate them, but to keep the royal family of Amarna's subsequent locations a closely guarded secret.

As head of the Amarna family, high priest and founder of the Aten cult, the one held responsible for this debacle in Egyptian imperial history, it makes sense that Akhenaten would be re-buried in secret and in a separate location from his family. It would appear that most of the royal tombs at Amarna had been completed and used at some point. Akhenaten himself, Tiye, Nefertiti, Meketaten and other children had initially been buried at Amarna, but clearly their bodies were moved elsewhere out of necessity. However, the grave of Akhenaten's oldest daughter Meritaten, at Amarna, was never used and that of her husband Smenkhkare has yet to be found, so it seems. It appears that a tomb for the youngest son, Tutankhaten (Tutenkhamun), was either never started at Amarna, or not completed. Famously, he was buried at Thebes, in a tomb that was largely unadulterated by grave robbers - a discovery that still reverberates around the world today.

Within a short time, the entire city of Amarna was abandoned, after the death of Tutenkhamun. Further-more the city was ransacked and the statues and temples damaged or destroyed. Many of the Stelae were defaced, knocked over and buried or hidden. Thankfully, due to a very unrigorous and obviously hurried defacing and abandonment of the city of Akhetaten, there is much remaining that has enabled us to tell the story of Akhenaten and his family. Being located on the western edge of the eastern desert the city was soon enough buried in sand, forgotten and hidden from us for a very long time. For millennia this Pharaoh, his religious heresy and his shining capital city were completely forgotten by Egyptians and the wider world, until the age of archaeology plucked his existence from underneath the sands.

THE BOY KING - TUTANKHATEN

Of course the most famous Pharaoh of all time, is the short reigning Tutankhaten, known to the world as Tutenkhamun. He did not become Pharaoh immediately after the death of his father, that fell to the also short-lived Smenkhkare, husband of oldest daughter Meritaten.

We will return to Meritaten and what happened to her soon, but part of that story is told by what befell her youngest sibling - Neb Kheperu Ra (Nebkheperure), meaning "The master of the manifestations of Ra", but his royal official name was Tutankhaten, which he was crowned as. Like his other siblings, he was named by his father in honour of the Aten, meaning "Living image of the Aten". It was not expected that he would ever become Pharaoh, being the youngest child of the family, born to Akhenaten's second (and junior) wife Kiya.

The death of both Akhenaten and Smenkhkare was sudden and unexpected, leaving Tutankhaten as the next Pharaoh, at just 8 years old, around 1332 BCE. It may seem bizarre by today's standards, but the Pharaoh was expected to have a wife, and to strengthen his legitimacy he was married to his half-sister Ankhesepaaten (later known as Ankhesenamun), continuing the royal bloodline. It is most likely that the marriage happened after the death of Smenkhkare, prior to coronation of Tutankhaten, but it may have happened earlier, we have no records to prove the date.

The royal couple, clearly some years later, had two daughters, both of whom died in infancy. At the beginning of Tutankhaten's reign the royal court remained at Amarna, and evidence from his tomb shows that the Aten was still recognised as a major deity. However it seems that he made a fairly rapid move to reconcile the unpopular Atenism with the traditional Egyptian religion, in particular the cult of Amum-Ra and the Amun priesthood, that his father had abandoned. As a result of this decision activity at Amarna decreased and around the 4th year of his reign he made a complete break with both Amarna (the city of Akhetaten) and Atenism.

At this time, Tutankhaten moved his royal court back to the traditional place of Memphis, leaving the city of Amarna (Akhetaten) completely. Also he restored the polytheistic form of traditional Egyptian religion to its former place, with Amun-Ra reinstated as the chief deity of Egypt. Tutankhaten's restoration of the old religion was recorded on the Restoration Stele and the cult of the god Amun, primarily located at Thebes was restored to prominence by this stele.

In addition to this, the royal couple changed their names to "Tutankhamun" and "Ankhesenamun", reflecting this sea-change, by the replacement of the suffix 'Aten' with 'Amun'. This was as clear a symbol of the rejection of Atenism and the acceptance of Amun-Ra as the primary god of Egypt as anyone could make. It was probably necessary, given his weak position as Pharaoh. As one of his first acts, Tutankhamun re-established diplomatic relations with the Mitanni and carried out military campaigns in Nubia (to the south) and also in the Near East. Probably at the start of his reign, construction of a royal tomb in the Valley of The Kings (near Thebes) began, together with an accompanying mortuary temple. However, due to Tutankhamun's untimely death neither were finished.

So, from year 4, aged around 12 to 13 years old, Tutankhamun completely reversed both the religious and political policies of his father and of his older, supposed, half-brother/relative Smenkhkare. His tomb contained extensive military armaments, such as bows, khopesh swords, daggers, wrist-guards, maces, shields and a club, suggesting he had extensive weaponry training, but given his young age, it is unlikely that he participated in many of his military campaigns, if any at all. Whether he took up arms or not, Tutankhamun's military reign was undefeated, and two victorious battles with Nubians and Asiatics were recorded on the walls of his mortuary temple at Thebes.

Figure 17: Statue of a Lion re-inscribed by Tutankhamun found in Sudan (1390-1352 BCE). This is one of a pair of Lions made for Amenhotep III, but which was re-inscribed by his grandson. Tutankhamun claimed to have renewed the temple erected by his grandfather, presumably as part of the reinstatement of the cult of Amun (held by the British Museum).

Tutankhamun was one of the few kings to be worshipped as a deity during his own lifetime. A stele discovered at Karnak, that was dedicated to Amun-Ra and Tutankhamun, indicated that the Pharaoh could be appealed to in his deified state. Temples of the cult of Tutankhamun were built as far away as Kawa (in modern Sudan) and Farasin Nubia. One can presume that he was afforded this honour by the priesthood of Amun-Ra in exchange for, or perhaps in recognition of, his restoration of the traditional religion, in particular the return of the old priesthood of Amun and elevation of Amun-Ra to his former position as chief deity.

Reused Funerary Goods

According to Nicholas Reeves, almost 80% of Tutankhamun's burial equipment was derived from a royal woman's original funerary goods, including the famous gold mask, middle coffin, canopic coffinettes, several of the gilded shrine panels, the shabti-figures, the boxes and chests, the royal jewellery, etc., and adapted for use after his unexpected early death. He suggests it was Neferneferuaten's burial equipment, but equally it may have been that of Meritaten, who herself appears to have become confused with Neferneferuaten. To me it seems more likely that they were the grave good intended for Meritaten, given that she was not buried in Egypt. There is no record of her death in Egypt and the 'reign of Neferneferuaten' is extremely tenuous/unproven, if indeed there was such an individual who became an interim Pharaoh.

In 2015, Reeves published evidence showing that an earlier cartouche found on Tutankhamun's famous gold mask reads,

"Ankheperure mery-Neferkheperure" or (Ankheperure beloved of Akhenaten). It would appear that the mask originally was made for Nefertiti, Akhenaten's Great Royal Wife, who used the royal name Ankheperure, but as she had died this title was also attributed to Meritaten. It could therefore be referring to either Nefertiti or Meritaten. Given that Nefertiti had died relatively long ago, during Akhenaten's reign, it most likely belonged to the now disappeared and unaccounted for Meritaten.

This information implies that either Neferneferuaten/Meritaten was deposed in a struggle for power, possibly deprived of a royal burial as a Pharaoh, or that she was buried elsewhere or even not buried in Egypt at all. If she has left the kingdom, her funerary goods would have become redundant and could conveniently be adapted for Tutankhamun, in advance of his death. The expense of creating funerary goods was immense and one can only assume that it made good financial sense to adapt those of another family member (that were no longer needed) than to dispose of them.

One researcher notes that Tutankhamun's tomb follows a traditional architectural design feature that suggests that the tomb had been built for a female person (chamber to the right instead of the usual left side). Considered with other evidence, this supports the tomb being that of a female royal that was unused and thus could be adapted for the burial of Tutankhamun, along with the reuse of female funerary goods and other artefacts.

A Death in Mysterious Circumstances

Instead of a long and glorious reign, Tutankhamun died unexpectedly at the age of 18 (possibly 19). The suggested date of his death is circa 1323 BCE. In 2010 scientists found traces of

Figure 18: The gold funeral mask of Pharaoh Tutankhamun (held by the Egyptian Museum in Cairo. Photograph by Helena Zacharias).

malaria parasites in his mummified remains and posited that malaria in combination with degenerative bone disease may have been the cause of death. However, there has been much speculation as to his cause of death. Some suspect that he was murdered or died from malaria or some other fatal disease. Others have suggested that Tutankhamun's chest (which is missing ribs and a sternum) might have been crushed in an accident, such as falling from his chariot.

The most recent study suggests Tutankhamun had necrosis of the bone and a possible clubfoot, which may have meant that he used canes to assist him in walking. Neither the canes nor his sandals show the kinds of wear that would be expected if that were true, but it is likely such items would be brand new for a royal burial. Some believe that he is most likely to have died of complications from a broken leg, possibly compounded by malaria. It is possible that he had a gangrene infection from the leg injury, which may well have killed him. If indeed he had fallen from a chariot, or had some other accident - it might explain the broken leg, missing ribs, crushed chest and ultimately his death. The theory of murder by a blow to the head was arrived at as a result of the 1968 X-ray which showed two bone fragments inside his skull. This theory, it is claimed, was more or less disproved by further analysis of the X-rays and a CT scan. Even so, loose skull fragments could still be either from the age of the skull or from a blow. The inter-cranial bone fragments were determined to be the result of the modern unwrapping of the mummy (in 1968) as they are loose and not fixed to the embalming resin. No evidence of bone thinning or calcified membranes, possibly indicative of a fatal blow to the head, was found, but even so it is hard to entirely dismiss this as a possibility, even if a remote one.

Four extravagant chariots, disassembled, were found in the tomb, along with a further two in the annex. Clearly chariot riding was important to Tutenkhamun, and one must wonder, considering his chest injuries and broken leg, is a chariot accident the most likely cause of death? Dr Alfred Jones suggests that he may have been murdered by Aye, his advisor and successor. While this seems plausible he might equally have been murdered by powerful followers of Amun-Ra, who wished to obliterate what little was left of Akhenaten's family and legacy. It would appear that, from his grave goods, Tutenkhamun had not entirely abandoned Atenism, even if in public he appeared to have done so.

In addition to his devotion to the Aten, as well as Amun, Tutenkhamun had kept his father's city entirely in tact. Although the royal family and entourage had moved away from the city of Akhetaten, Tutenkhamun had made no efforts to destroy it or erase the temples and writings related to either Akhenaten or the Aten. Amarna was not used as a capital or for anything at all under Tutenkhamun's reign, but it remained there, as a constant reminder of the heretical Akhentaten and his unpopular Aten cult. This in itself must have made Tutenkhamun unpopular with some of the government, all of the priesthood of Amun and as a result of his inaction on this matter, perhaps he was considered unreliable or untrustworthy?

So there would certainly have been sufficient enemies and sufficient cause for people to wish to do away with the young Pharaoh. What better cover for a murder could one find than a chariot accident? Careful sabotage of a vehicle that could travel at 25-30 mph would easily lead to major injuries or death, particularly for a Pharaoh who was already in poor physical health. Some suggest that Aye plotted his death but of course this is only speculation.

Whether he died of malaria, a bone infection, a chariot accident, chariot tampering or a direct murder, his reign was suddenly cut short, and before his tomb was completed. As a result, he was buried in a tomb that, although designed for a female, had originally been prepared for Aye, who would soon after become his successor, Aye II, by marriage with Tutankhanun's young widow (and sister) Ankhesenamun. After 2 minor robberies, probably shortly after his burial, the tomb was accidentally covered up. Much of the valley, including the entrance to Tutankhamun's tomb, was covered by a layer of alluvium over which huts were later built for the tomb workers who cut KV57, in which Pharaoh Horemheb was buried. Further rubble from the digging of nearby tombs for Ramesses V and VI, made the tomb even more inaccessible for over 2000 years, until it was found by Howard Carter in November 1922.

It is also interesting to note that Horemheb, who served as one of Tutankhamun's chief advisers, went on to become Pharaoh himself, after the death of Aye II. Like Aye before him, he married Tutenkhamun's widow/sister - Ankhesenamun. Horemheb was not related to Akhenaten in any way, and so brought an end to the dynasty, and not only that, he began to erase Akhenaten and his family from history.

Like other rulers associated with the Amarna period - Akhenaten, Smenkhkare, and Aye, Tutenkhamun was to suffer the fate of having his name stricken from some later king lists.

However, he was not systematically erased like his father. Many of his monuments were usurped, as were those of Akhenaten, Smenkhkare and Aye, mostly by Horemheb, soon after he became Pharaoh. Horemheb demolished much of the state capital of Amarna (Akhetaten), reusing the rubble in his own building projects, before leaving the sands to cover it over.

Many stelae were defaced, statues defaced or damaged, the graves of the royal family were ransacked and temples obliterated. Clearly those looking for their revenge on the cult of the Aten were finally able to taste it, albeit served cold. This had become possible now that the last blood relative Pharaoh of Akhenaten was dead. Akhenaten's one remaining daughter, Ankhesenamun, was kept alive as a pawn, supposedly to give some form of legitimacy to both Aye and then Horemheb, being of the royal bloodline. However, even she did not last long into Horemheb's reign.

We do not know how she died, whether it was of natural causes or murder, as no official record was made of her death. Horemheb himself ruled for around 25 years and presumably had no surviving sons, despite marriage to three wives. Given the lack of male progeny, Horemheb appointed his vizier Paramesse as his successor, before his death in 1292 BCE. Parmesse assumed the throne as Ramesses I, ending the disastrous closing chapters of the 18th dynasty and beginning the 19th dynasty.

MERITATEN - AKHENATEN'S DAUGHTER

Of his children, there are many references to his eldest daughter, Meritaten, also known by her 'pet name' of Mayati. She was born approximately 1356 BCE but it has been suggested as late as 1352 BCE. Her name means "The beloved of Aten". She was the first child of Pharaoh Amenhotep IV (later Akhenaten) and his Great Royal Wife, Nefertiti. She was the first of six sisters born of Akhenaten and Nefertiti - Meritaten, Meketaten, Ankhesenpaaten, Neferneferuaten Tasherit, Neferneferure and Setepenre. Her most famous sibling, a half-brother through second Queen Kiya, was Tutankhaten (Tutenkhamun), who I have already discussed, in the previous chapter.

Early Years

Meritaten, who was the eldest daughter of the then Amenhotep IV and Nefertiti, already appears in the very early monuments at Karnak. She is the only princess who appears in these early scenes and is shown accompanying her mother Nefertiti. She was most likely born in the first or second year of her father's reign, in the city of Thebes, on the western bank of the Nile, in the palace of Malquatta. The remaining five sisters, and her half-brother (Tutankhaten/Tutenkhamun) were all born in the new capital city of Akhenaten (Amarna). Meritaten may well have been 3-5 years old when Akhenaten moved his family, government and entourage to Amarna. She is depicted on all of the boundary stelae, in Akhenaten (Amarna) from year 5 onwards, of his reign. She most definitely was still a small girl when the city was being constructed and the royal family moved to the new capital city, from lower Egypt to this relatively obscure place.

During the first 14 years of Akhentaten's reign, Meritaten was the second lady of the court and the most important woman in the country, after her mother, Nefertiti. She appears in countless representations, accompanied by her parents and sometimes also by her younger sisters. There are numerous sculptures of both her and her sisters, which are very stylised, like the two-dimensional images, due to the elongated, oval shape of their heads.

Figure 19: A fragment of a limestone stela depicting one of Akhenaten's daughters. This may well be Meritaten, but as the corresponding cartouche is missing, it is not possible to definitively identify her (held by the British Museum).

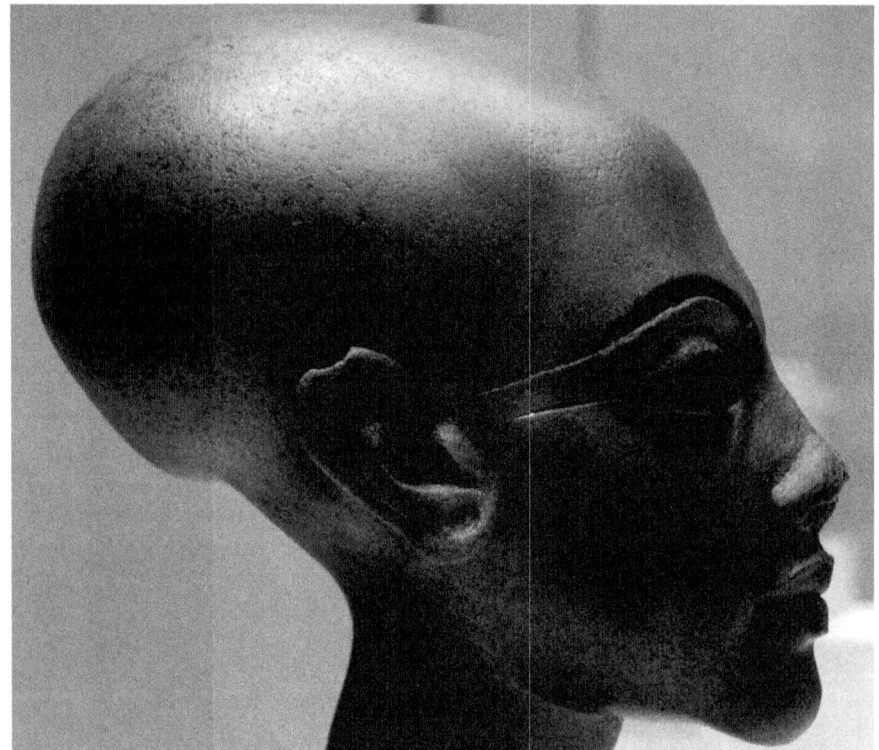

Figure 20: Red quartzite head of Meritaten. Note that given the head is shaved, as was common for royal children, she would have been quite young at the time that this was made (held by the Egyptian Museum of Berlin collection. Photograph by Miguel Hermoso Cuesta).

Life at Amarna must have been rather sad for the young princess (and indeed her whole family) - following the tragic death of Tiye (Akhenaten's mother) her grandmother, her next oldest sister Meketaten died. An image in Akhenaten's tomb clearly shows Meritaten with her sisters Neferneferuaten and Ankhesenpaaten in mourning Tiye's death, around year 13 or 14 of Akhenaten's reign. Her younger sisters Neferneferure and Setepenre are not present in this scene. Sadly, within a year, the surviving daughters lost their beloved mother, Nefertiti too.

It is at this time that Meritaten was elevated to Akhenaten's successor and consort. In a 'mara' or viewing temple, within the Amarna complex inscriptions of the Great Queen Nefertiti's name were carefully erased and replaced by that of Meritaten, the eldest daughter. In the actual images, according to Cyril Aldred:

"Nefertiti's distinctive attributes had been blotted out with cement, her features recut and her head enlarged to the dropsical cranium of the Princess Royal."

However, more recent analysis indicates that it may well have been the second Queen, Kiya, whose name was replaced by Meritaten.

Figure 21: Red quartzite relief of two princesses in their chariot. From River Palace (room 25), Amarna. This relief shows a procession of chariots, the one on the right carrying princesses Meritaten and Meketaten riding across the city (held by the British Museum).

Similar alterations are found throughout the city of Akhetaten, with Meritaten taking on the royal and political roles of her deceased mother, although the reasoning behind why Akhentaten did this is unclear. Meritaten was raised to the position of Great Royal Wife sometime during the later years of Akhenaten's reign. It is even possible that she served as Akhenaten's Queen, but this is by no means certain. During the later years of Akhenaten's reign Nefertiti disappears from the scene, recorded as deceased, and it seems that Meritaten took over the role as leading royal lady at court. The Maru-Aten was rededicated. This sunshade/temple used to belong to the royal beloved Kiya (who also died), but her image was adapted everywhere for Meritaten. Due to the adaption of the monuments it's not entirely clear if young girls by the name of Meritaten-tasherit ("Meritaten-junior") and Ankhesenpaaten-tasherit ("Ankhesenpaaten-junior") are daughters of Kiya or if these girls are possibly the young children of Meritaten.

Clearly she was an important figure within the Amarna dynasty but still much mystery remains about her. The texts of the boundary stele mention that Meritaten was meant to be buried at Akhetaten (Amarna):

"Let a tomb be made for me in the eastern mountain of Akhetaten. Let my burial be made in it, in the millions of jubilees which the Aten, my father, has decreed for me. Let the burial of the Great King's Wife, Nefertiti, be made in it, in the millions of years which the Aten, my father, decreed for her. Let the burial of the King's Daughter, Meritaten, [be made] in it, in these millions of years."

The royal tombs in Amarna were used for the burial of Queen Nefertiti, second daughter Meketaten, Akhenaten's mother Tiye and Akhenaten himself, and most likely were closed after the death and burial of Akhenaten. After that, Meritaten's burial would most likely have been planned for one of the other royal tombs in the Amarna area. Empty tombs have been found, in an unfinished state, one of which was presumably for her. So if she had somehow disappeared from the scene, it would make sense that her proposed tomb was unused, her funerary goods remained unused and her body was not to be found anywhere in Egypt.

Marriage to Smenkhkare

Meritaten is known to have married Smenkhkare. Almost nothing is known about his origins, apart from a few mentions of him in the Amarna letters. It is assumed that he was a member of the royal family, possibly being Akhenaten's son, but very little about him or his lineage can be ascertained. Given Meritaten's elevated status, it is expected that her husband Smenkhkare would receive the throne of Egypt, gaining legitimacy through Meritaten, his Great Royal Wife, oldest daughter of Akhenaten. It is possible that they had one or two children together - Meritaten-tasherit ("Meritaten-junior") and Ankhesenpaaten-tasherit ("Ankhesenpaaten-junior") but this is unclear, possibly a confusion with daughters of Meritaten's step-mother Kiya. Meritaten-tasherit is suggested to have lived 1351 - 1295 BCE. Before her marriage to Smenkhkare and his short reign, Meritaten's titles are given as: *"King's Daughter of his body, his beloved, Great King's Wife.* Her full title on some Amarna monuments is given as *"King's Daughter of his body, his beloved Meritaten, born of the great royal wife, his beloved, Lady of the Two Lands (Neferneferuaten)| may she live."*

Reign of Confusion

After the death of her father, in his 17th year of his reign, it would appear that Neferneferuaten became Pharaoh, a younger daughter of Akhenaten and Nefertiti. However, this seems to go completely against any Egyptian royal practice, and may be a confusion of what happened in the succession.

According to Egyptian-Greek historian Manetho's 'Epitome', "Akenkeres" is recorded to have assumed the throne for herself as the female king Neferneferuaten. Neferneferuaten is assigned a reign of 2 years and 1 month and is placed in Manetho's account as the immediate predecessor of "Rathothis", who is believed to be Tutankhamun. It is possible that there is confusion between who these people were - "Akenkeres" quite possibly being Meritaten.

Manetho's 'Epitome', a summary of his work, described the 18th dynasty succession as Orus or "Amenophis for 30 years 10 months." After Orus, who is most likely Amenhotep III, comes: "his daughter Acencheres for 12 years 1 month, then her brother "Rathothis" for 9 years". According to Marc Gabolde, "Acencheres" is "Ankhkheperure" with a transcription error converting 2 years, 1 month into the 12 years.

Akhenaten is not even mentioned in the most accurate 18th dynasty king list of Manetho's 'Epitome', compiled by Josephus in his polemical work 'Against Apion'. Most agree that "Rathothis" likely refers to Tutankhamun; therefore, the succession order also supports "Acencheres" as "Ankhkheperure". Strangely, Manetho states that "Rathothis" is followed by "his son "Acencheres" for 12 years 5 months, his son "Acencheres II" for 12 years 3 months", which demonstrates the limits to which Manetho may be relied upon for accuracy about the Amarna period.

It is suggested that Smenkhkare ruled as co-regent with Akhenaten shortly before his death, which would be indicative that he was to replace Akhenaten, ruling with Akhentaten's first daughter (Meritaten) alongside him. To me this makes more sense than an intermediate (and very short) reign by Neferneferuaten, who had scant mention anywhere and appeared to be of no importance at all. Unlike Smenkhkare, there are no known named depictions of Neferneferuaten; she is only securely attested in inscriptions.

J.P. Allen suggests that Neferneferuaten followed Akhenaten and that upon her death, Smenkhkare ascended as Pharaoh. Allen proposes that following Nefertiti's death in Year 13 or 14, that she became Pharaoh Neferneferuaten. After Neferneferuaten's short rule, according to Allen, Smenkhkare became Pharaoh. In this theory, both Pharaohs succeeded Akhenaten: Neferneferuaten as the chosen successor and Smenkhkare as a rival with the same praenomen.

Work on the Amarna tombs is believed to have halted shortly after year 13 of Akhenaten's reign. However, in the tomb of Merire we see Smenkhkare and his Great Royal Wife Meritaten handing out rewards to Merire. The scene is rather non-standard in the fact that the royal couple is depicted standing before the window of appearance. They seem to be standing at the same level as the court official instead of the more traditional depiction where they appear in the window and are shown handing down gifts. One can assume that the depiction of Smenkhkare in Merire's tomb must date to no later than year

13 or 14. For him to have succeeded Neferneferuaten means that aside from a lone wine docket, he left not a single trace over the course of five to six years, although both Smenkhkare and Meritaten are mentioned in the Amarna Letters from the last 4 years of Akhenaten's reign.

Another theory, put forward by Marc Gabolde has suggested that Smenkhkare's Great Royal Wife, Meritaten, became Pharaoh Neferneferuaten after her husband's death. The main argument against this is a box from Tutankhamun's tomb that lists Akhenaten, Neferneferuaten, and Meritaten as three separate individuals. There, Meritaten is explicitly listed as Great Royal Wife. Further, various private stelae depict the 'female Pharaoh' with Akhenaten. However in this theory, Akhenaten would be dead by the time Meritaten became Pharaoh as Neferneferuaten. Gabolde suggests that these depictions are retrospective. Yet, as these are private cult stelae, it would require a number of people to get the same idea to commission a retrospective, commemorative stele at the same time. Allen notes that the everyday interaction portrayed in them more likely indicates two living people rather than the one person.

So, clearly there is confusion over whether Neferneferuaten was Pharaoh, whether this person was actually Smenkhkare or Meritaten or some other individual. With confusing use of names and titles and lack of any really hard evidence, a lot of the theories are conjecture, especially as much of the record was either lost or destroyed. What is certain is that Smenkhkare and Meritaten ruled Egypt until the untimely death of Smenkhkare in 1334 BCE.

Disappearance of Meritaten

It is not known what happened to Meritaten after the death of her husband Smenkhkare, she just disappears from history. There are no known funerary goods inscribed with her name that have ever surfaced and it would appear that her funerary goods, prepared long in advance, were repurposed for her younger half-brother Tutankhaten/Tutankhamun. There is no official record of her death anywhere in Egypt, she seems to have disappeared from the scene at roughly the same time as her husband Smenkhkare died.

The last evidence of Meritaten seems to appear however in the tomb of Tutankhamun. Between the paws of the statue of Anubis lay a scribal palette that had once belonged to Meritaten. Her name also appears on a box along with the name of her husband Smenkhkare.

At this point, approximately 1334 BCE, Meritaten disappears from Egyptian life and from the records in Egypt. No occupied tomb has been found, only an unfinished tomb that was probably hers. Above all, no body has been found, nor any record of her funeral or burial in Egypt. So what happened to Meritaten? For clues to what happened to her, we need to look beyond Egypt, to the West.

Aye II and Horemheb - the End of a Dynasty

We know for certain that Smenkhkare and Meritaten ruled as Pharaoh and Great Royal Wife (or perhaps jointly) until 1334 BCE. Tutankhaten became Pharaoh in 1332 BCE and soon after changed his name to Tutankhamun, long before his death in 1324 BCE. What is clear is that Aye II succeeded

Tutankhamun around 1324 BCE, ruling for approximately 4 years. He was a General and not of the royal bloodline, but by marrying one of Akhenaten's daughters (Tutankhamun's widow and half-sister, born as Ankhesenpaaten), he had a legitimate claim to the throne of Egypt. His reign was short, perhaps because he was already of advanced age when he became Pharaoh. Aye II was then succeeded by Horemheb, who became the husband of Queen Ankhesenamun (formerly Ankhesenpaaten and widow for a second time), thus legitimising his claim to the throne. Ankhesenamun, who like her brother had changed her name to remove all reference to the Aten, was Tutankhamun's sister or half-sister and had for unknown reasons married the elderly Aye II, outliving him to become wife of the next Pharaoh.

Horemheb was not a blood relative of any of his predecessors. It is thought that another General, Nakhtmin was the chosen successor of Aye II, indeed he was heir to the throne during Aye's reign, but he clearly did not become Pharaoh. No records exist regarding his death - it is possible that he died during Aye's reign or that he was murdered by Horemheb so that he could usurp the throne. Another man was also given the title "Hereditary Prince", Nay, but he was perhaps not named as a successor, as his tomb survived undesecrated unlike that of Nakhtmin, the acknowledged "Crown Prince". Aye's attempts to sideline Horemheb failed, and unsurprisingly Aye II was perhaps the most 'punished' of the previous Pharaohs. Horemheb made a fair attempt at expunging the names of his immediate predecessors, especially Aye II, from the historical record, but it was not entirely successful.

Figure 22: Limestone statue of Horembeb (before he became Pharaoh) with his first wife Amenia, dated from the time when he was Commander-in-Chief of the Egyptian army (held by the British Museum).

As noted earlier, Aye II's original tomb was not destroyed, it was most likely overlooked, leading to the preservation of 'The Hymn to the Aten'. No doubt Horemheb would have destroyed it had he known of its whereabouts, as he took great pains to destroy all known references to Aye II, even in previous reigns, when he served Akhenaten and Tutankhamun. Horemheb desecrated Aye's final tomb (near Luxor) and had most of Aye's royal cartouches erased while his sarcophagus was smashed into numerous fragments. Surprisingly, the intact sarcophagus lid was discovered by American archaeologist Otto Schaden in 1972. The lid had probably been removed at the start of the destruction and was most likely buried under debris from the devastation and so forgotten - hence it still bore Aye's cartouche. Horemheb also usurped the mortuary temple of Aye II (at Medinet Habu on the opposite bank near Luxor) for his own use - erasing Aye's name everywhere and having all references to him replaced with his own name.

No objects belonging to Horemheb were found in Tutankhamun's tomb, but items among the tomb goods (donated by other high ranking officials), were found - such as those from Overseer of the Treasuries Maya and General Nakhtmin, were clearly identified by Egyptologists. However, Professor of Egyptology at Kanazawa University, Nozomu Kawai claims that Horemheb was an active participant at Tutankhamun's burial, based on the wall scene of the tomb, in which Horemheb may be among the group of men dragging Tutankamun's coffin.

Horemheb was of common birth but he became an important General during the Amarna period. His first marriage was to Amenia but it seems that she died during Aye's reign. By

Figure 23: Limestone relief of Pharaoh Horemheb's coronation, from inside his tomb at Saqqara, 30km south of modern Cairo (Saqqara, Egypt. Photograph by Helena Zacharias).

marrying Aye's widow, Ankhesenamun, Horemheb was able to become Pharaoh legitimately. It appears that Ankhesenamun may have died early on in Horemheb's reign and that Horemheb remarried once again. His first 3rd marriage was to Mutnedjmet, who is suggested as Nefertiti's sister. This would once again give legitimacy to his reign as she would be related to a former Queen of the Amarna dynasty. It has also been suggested that she was the daughter of Aye II, the previous Pharaoh. Whether or not she was a relative of Nefertiti or Aye, Mutnedjmet became Horemheb's 'Great Royal Wife'. She died in the 13th year of his reign, leaving no children.

It is now acknowledged that he obliterated images of all of the Amarna Pharaohs and destroyed and vandalised as many of the buildings and monuments associated with them as he could. As Horemheb had no surviving children his reign marks the end of the 18th dynasty of Egypt. His main act seems to have been to restore the previous order of things - the power of the priesthood of Amun and the traditional way of life that had existed under Amenhotep III and earlier Pharaohs. In doing so Horemheb was keen to destroy Amarna city, the temples of the Aten all over Egypt, the tombs of Akhenaten and his family and to erase all mention of Akhenaten and his progeny. He didn't do a very careful job in Amarna, which is why we have so much information about Akhenaten and his progeny. Until the city at Amarna was rediscovered, the whole Amarna period was largely shrouded in mystery, and in most cases, completely forgotten by history. The one exception of suffering Horemheb's full wrath was Tutankhamun. Although Horemheb removed him from the king list, he didn't destroy all of Tutankhamun's monuments or buildings. However, Horemheb's wife Ankhesenamun (widow and sister of Tutankhamun) is barely visible during the final years of the 18th dynasty.

Having no surviving sons, Horemheb appointed his Visier, Paramesse, as his successor, seemingly to reward Paramesse's loyalty and also because Paramesse had both a son and grandson to secure the royal succession of Egypt. After a long reign, Horemheb died in 1292 BCE, leaving Paramesse to become Pharaoh as Ramesses I, who was to become one the most famous names among Pharaohs. Upon assuming the throne, Ramesses I founded the 19th dynasty, which was the 2nd dynasty in the New Kingdom era of Egypt. And thus ended the 18th dynasty, the final years of which were mired by disgrace, hatred and ultimately erasure from history.

THE FLIGHT TO SPAIN

The events of Egypt are recorded in the official writings of the Egyptians in hieroglyphs and images and also of their neighbours, usually in cuneiform. These have a chronology and, although they may have a level of bias, or even on occasion contain some lies, they are generally reliable historical documents. The preceding chapter gives a fair picture of the events of the Amarna dynasty, based upon these writings. Once we leave the shores of Egypt we run into trouble. From here on we are reliant on unverified and largely unreliable sources.

One such source, is the Irish collection 'Lebor Gabála Érenn' (The Book of Invasions), which is comprised of three rather different parallel versions of Irish history. This book, at least in part was probably begun in the 7th century CE, so it is much older than the Scottish chronicles we have. The earliest copy extant is from the 11th century. The differing versions call the characters by different names at times, causing much confusion, but it is from this work that we find the more complete story of the man who married and rescued the Pharaoh's daughter, known here as Scotia:

"Second Redaction

What is the true story of the Sons of Míl? [Their origin is] a people that is in the mountain of Armenia, called Hiberi. They had a famous king Míl s. Bile s. Nema. He was holding the kingship against his father's brother, Refloir s Bile; and he came with four ships' companies a voyaging... They had three other months upon the sea, and at last reached Egypt at the end of 1354 years after the first Taking of Ireland by Partholón; 914 years after the drowning of

Pharaoh in the Red Sea. They reached Egypt. Pharaoh Nectanebus was king of Egypt at that time, and he was the 45th king after Pharaoh Cenchres, who was drowned in the Red Sea...

He it is (Nectanebus) who was king of Egypt, to whom Míl s Bile came with his expedition and he [Míl] found a welcome there for a space of 8 years, and he [the king] gave him his daughter Scotia."

This account differs greatly from the other 'pseudo-histories', with a vastly different placing in time and entirely different names of those involved. What it does have in common is a foreign ruler coming to Egypt, marrying the daughter of a Pharaoh and later leaving Egypt, with his Egyptian royal wife. It is interesting to note that according to author Angela Teryan, the ancestral land of the Indo-Europeans was Armenia since the 7th millennium BCE, which was many times larger than the current country of Armenia, reaching into what is today southern Turkey and Northern Syria. The southern part of what once was Armenia corresponds exactly with the location of Mitani, eastern Hitti (Hittites) and northern Phoenicia.

It would appear to me that there are some elements of truth within the 'pseudo-histories' but given the multitude of sources, rewriting and embellishments, the narrative could have been utterly corrupted over time. The Irish text confuses things further with the Alexandrian rule of Egypt being given as the reason for Míl and his people leaving the country:

"Thereafter a royal city was founded by Alexander Egypt, Alexandria by name, and the native rule of Egypt was then taken away, and the Greeks took authority therein; and the rule of

Egypt was in the possession of the Greeks of Alexandria from that onward. So it is then that Míl came from Egypt to his own people."

The Scottish texts use ancient sources from the 'Old World' but they were compiled much later than the 'Lebor Gabála Érenn'. According to the book the 'Scotichronicon', written around 1435 CE, by Walter Bower (the Abbot of Inchcolm Abbey), from Scotland, using Latin:

"In ancient times, Scota, the daughter of pharaoh, left Egypt with her husband Gaythelos by name and a large following. For they had heard of the disasters which were going to come upon Egypt, and so through the instructions of the gods they fled from certain plagues that were to come. They took to the sea, entrusting themselves to the guidance of the gods"

"… After sailing for many days over the sea with troubled minds, they were finally glad to put their boats in at a certain shore because of bad weather."

These statements immediately raise the questions: who was Gaythelos? Was he the same person as Míl? Did Meritaten marry this man in Egypt? Did they flee Egypt together? Where did they go to?

Bower went on to state that the 'certain shore' was northern Britain, and that Scota and Gaythelos and their followers eventually settled in what is now Scotland for a while, until being forced to flee to Ireland. The original sources for Bower's account of Scota and Gaythelos was certainly, in part, the work of John of Fordun, and may also have been the 'World Chronicle' compiled by the Roman writer Eusebius of Caesarea, around

320 CE, based upon the earlier 'History of Egypt' compiled by the Greek writer Euhemerus. Of course, he may have used extracts from Egyptian-Greek historian Manetho's 'Epitome', from around 300 BCE.

Princess Meritaten may have taken a Gael prince as her husband after the death of Smenkhkare, but we cannot be sure. In a nutshell, this woman, known to us as Scotia/Scota is thought to have secured a passage from Egypt, ended up in Spain, where she married for the second time (or was married while still in Egypt) and eventually, with her husband, sailed to Britain and Ireland.

Early Maritime Ventures

Some academics have claimed that for Meritaten to travel to Britain and Ireland would have been impossible in the late 14th century BCE. However, there are many indications that this may have been a difficult journey, but not one that was impossible.

The earliest known seagoing voyages are those of the Polynesian peoples, known as the Austronesian expansion, which took place a very long way from Egypt, in the Pacific Ocean. This is argued to have commenced from around 3000 BCE, which is long before North Africa and Europe were able to produce seagoing ships. Around the Mediterranean region rudimentary rafts, and later on ships, were used as early as 4000 BCE in Egypt but they were only suitable for navigating the River Nile. From the remains of clay tablets and containers, historians know that, from around 3500 BCE onwards, the Mesopotamians were building boats of reeds coated with tar or of wooden frames that were supported by inflated skins.

In Egypt improvements in ship building were significant. After a discovery in 1991, excavations began in 2000 of 14 boats at a royal burial site in Abydos, about 450 km south of Cairo. Remains at the site indicate the boat was associated with Pharaohs of the first dynasty and second dynasty, beginning about 3000 BCE. While these were Nile boats they were some 25m long and could accommodate 30 rowers.

Egypt is credited with the development of planking, which enabled sea voyages. The Minoans are regarded as the first seafaring people, followed by the Mycenaeans and Phoenicians. By around 2000 BCE the Minoans had warships and these galleys were propelled primarily by oars, with some small sails, fully wind powered ship were a much later development. The ships were probably built of planking, an Egyptian technique that they had improved upon. Actual warships in Egypt were constructed during the Middle Kingdom at the latest, but were first mentioned and described in some detail from 16th century BCE.

This text is written in the tomb KV39 in the Valley of the Kings, which is that of Amenhotep I (reigned 1526-1506 BCE).

"And I ordered to build twelve warships with rams, dedicated to Amun or Sobek or Maat and Sekhmet, whose image was crowned best bronze noses. Carport and equipped outside rook over the waters, for many paddlers, having covered rowers deck not only from the side, but and top. and they were on board eighteen oars in two rows on the top and sat on two rowers, and the lower – one, a hundred and eight rowers were. And twelve rowers aft worked on three steering oars. …and long ship seventy five cubits (41m), and the breadth sixteen, and in battle can go three-quarters of iteru per hour (about 6.5 knots)…"

Seafaring pre Late Bronze Age Collapse

The Late Bronze Age Collapse (LBAC) is regarded as a widespread societal collapse that occurred in the Mediterranean region, affecting Hellenistic (Greek) culture primarily from around 1100 BCE - 800 BCE or so, but it may have begun as early as the start of the 13th century BCE (according to academic Molly Greenhouse). It affected the Minoans and Mycenaeans particularly, but also affected the Mitanni, Hittites, Phoenicians and the Egyptians, to varying degrees. Prior to this series of unfortunate events, comprising the LBAC, the level of sophistication of seafaring, shipbuilding and trade was quite remarkable, as described in great detail by authors such as Shelley Wachsmann. The idea that technology and culture progresses in a linear fashion is false - at various times in human history there have been serious setbacks or 'dark ages'. The LBAC is one such instance of a major setback, that the Mediterranean region eventually recovered from, over a period of several centuries.

This would explain trade links between the Scandinavians and the Minoans being extant long prior to the Amarna period, probable links with the islands of Britain and Ireland too (according to Ukranian Professor Iurii Mosenkis). Such links disappeared, as evidenced by archaeological digs at ancient mines and were re-established, often at other locations, later on, at some time after the recovery in the Late Bronze Age.

An important iconographical document relating to Bronze Age shipbuilding was found in 1971, during the excavations at Akrotiri, on the volcanic island of Thera. In what is known as the "procession of ships", found in the fresco of the "West House", we see all the means of propulsion of the time: the sail, the oars supported on holepins and free paddling. The fresco dates from the middle of the 16th century BCE, which was a few years before the eruption of the volcano that destroyed the town of Akrotiri.

By the time of the Amarna period, ship building had become quite advanced and navigating the Mediterranean Sea was no longer a big problem, hence the existence of trade was already widespread. While hugging the coast was preferable to risking open waters, it was indeed possible to make long voyages, perhaps with multiple stops along the way.

The Minoans, Mycenaeans and Phoenicians were sea-going peoples, with trade connections beyond the Pillars of Hercules, so the idea of Meritaten being able to travel to Spain is completely feasible. Travelling from Spain to Britain would have been a lot more challenging but not impossible. Likewise travel from Northern Britain to Ireland would have been entirely possible, given the short distances. However, travel in the Irish Sea, the North Sea and the Atlantic Ocean would have been considerably risky, especially in winter time.

Some academics assume that long-distance travel didn't happen, it appears based on dismissing the idea of a multi-stage journey, however even today, many people undergo long journeys in two or more stages, so I would regard such dismissals as completely illogical.

Further rebuttal of the idea that early Bronze Age civilisations had not mastered the art of long-distance sailing is provided by the work of controversial Norwegian explorer Thor Heyerdahl. Heyerdahl's theory was that early civilisations were far more mobile than they are given credit for, and he spent most of his career replicating the traversing of trade routes in copies of ancient sea vessels.

Of great relevance to this period of Egyptian history is his two papyrus replica boats Ra I and Ra II. Ra I was built in Africa, at Lake Chad, using Ethiopian reeds, of the same type that ancient Egyptians would have used and based on drawings, inscriptions and models of boats from antiquity. Like its sister boat, Ra II was made from Ethiopian papyrus, but it was built in South America, at Lake Titicaca about a year later.

In 1969 Heyerdahl and his crew set off from Morocco in Ra I, hoping to reach the Americas. They discovered that a vital element of the Egyptian boatbuilding method had been forgotten - a tether that acted like a spring to keep the stern high in the water but that also offered greater flexibility. As a result of this omission, Ra I began to sag and break apart in heavy weather after successfully sailing more than 6,400 km. The crew was forced to abandon Ra I, some hundred miles (160 km) before the Caribbean islands and they carried on by yacht, with no casualties.

The following year, 1970, Ra II was completed and sent to Morocco, where (like its predecessor) it set sail across the Atlantic for the Americas. The boat became lost at sea and was famously the subject of a United Nations search and rescue mission. However, the boat and crew were not in any danger, having reached the Caribbean island of Barbados. Heyerdahl and his team, against scoffs of derision and disbelief, proved that ancient mariners could have made trans-Atlantic voyages by making use of the Canary Current that runs across the Atlantic. After Heyerdahl's triumph the Ra II was placed in the

Kon-Tiki Museum (named after another expedition) in Oslo, Norway, where it resides along with his other vessels. The book 'The Ra Expeditions' and the film documentary 'Ra', from 1972, followed Heyerdahl's unprecedented success.

Not only are the possibilities of ancient sea travel dismissed by many in academia, but the notion of cities and civilisations being older than we think is often dismissed too. Relatively recent discoveries, such as Göbekli Tepe, have shown that academic assumptions about civilisation being post 5000 BCE are completely wrong. It is also possible that origin stories that give older dates than academics believe to be true are not mere fabrications.

Origin stories are (according to Emeritus Reader in Classics, Henry Hurst of Cambridge University) quite likely fanciful, to give greater prestige to city states. However, he concedes that we have no way of proving their validity or falsehood, in the absence of archaeology to back it up. In the case of Carthage, a major city of the Pheonicians, it's origin is heavily disputed. The oldest date, 1218 BCE according to Philistus of Syracuse (Greek historian, c. 432 – 356 BCE), is often dismissed and the accepted traditional date is given as 814 BCE. However, more recent archaeological research would indicate that this is too early and could be perhaps at least 200 years prior. While this is quite a long time before the Amarna period, it does demonstrate the overly conservative attitude with regard to ancient accounts and the chronology of early civilisations, and their major centres. Archaeological estimates are almost always conservative and in some cases too conservative, which is particularly proven by recent finds in Turkey, Malta, the Americas and other locations around the world.

Seafaring post Late Bronze Age Collapse

The Mediterranean region began to recover from various destructive events, invasions of the 'Sea Peoples', trade/ economic crisis, wars and mass migrations, around 800 BCE, roughly speaking. So, now returning to the early maritime adventures of this period we see a re-emergence of more advanced shipbuilding and navigation. However, even with planked vessels, the open sea or ocean was extremely dangerous with ships of the era, and truly 'ocean going' vessels were not available until much later on, in the common era (CE). Accounts of incredible voyages, that are extant, can be attributed to the Phoenicians from the post LBAC later era.

For instance, Hanno, who was a Carthaginian explorer of the 5th Century BCE, explored the areas outside the Pillars of Hercules (Straits of Gibraltar), heading south to the west coast of Africa. He is believed to have reached as far as southern Morocco, but some historians, through analysis of Hanno's own descriptions of landmarks, believe that he may have reached as far south as Senegal & Gabon, which are in central Africa.

Himilco 'The Navigator', who was also from Carthage, is credited as the first 'Mediterranean' to sail to the shores of northern and north-western Europe in the late 6th BCE or possibly the early 5th Century BCE. According to later Roman writers, he sailed to both the islands of 'Albion', which we now call Britain and also to 'Ierne', which we know today as Ireland. These Phoenician (Carthaginian) voyagers may not be unique, but they are the only ones that we have written confirmation of. Indications are that trade occurred much earlier in the Late Bronze Age, including prior to the LBAC. Maybe these were the first people that were so notable that the Greeks and Romans were compelled to write of them, even though they were sworn enemies of Phoenicia and Carthage in particular.

Somewhat later again, 'On the Ocean', the account of Pytheas of Massalia (modern day Marseille in southern France), details his voyage of exploration to northern Europe in or around 325 BCE. The original work, which mentions the British Isles and the Arctic, is lost but the book has been mentioned by Strabo, Diodorus and others and marks the earliest known attempts at Oceanic travel.

Clearly long-distance travel by boat, most likely along coastal routes was possible in the Bronze Age, evidence would suggest as early as 2000 BCE. Presumably, voyagers would have made short trips in succession, i.e. multiple stop offs, for both safety and rationing reasons, as well as for the trading of goods. I see absolutely no reason why some Minoan/Mycenaean/Phoenician or even Hittite person of importance could not have come to Meritaten's aid and taken her away from Egypt by ship, or even via a flotilla/fleet of ships.

So, assuming that coastal travel beyond the Mediterranean Sea was possible, if Scotia/Meritaten made her way to Ireland via north-eastern Britain, some time after the death of her husband Smenkhkare, where did she go en-route? How did her departure from Egypt come about? It has been suggested that Meritaten wrote to various regional monarchs asking for help, i.e., an appeal to be rescued. It has been suggested that she appealed to and was helped by either the Hittites or the Phoenicians (a maritime people). The Hittites were enemies of Egypt and their empire, established around 1650 BCE, stretched across Turkey and down into what is now Lebanon, threatening Egyptian dominions and allies. Phoenicia was established around 1800 BCE and was spread out along Palestine and Lebanon and in city states, It later established the Punic empire around 800 BCE, based in Carthage in north-west Africa(modern Tunisia).

The Zannanza Affair

A discovery was made in the Hittite capital of Hattusa (now Boghaz Koy, in modern Turkey) - a letter inscribed on a badly damaged cuneiform tablet, that was a part of the annals of the Hittite king, Suppiluliuma I called 'The Deeds of Suppiluliuma' which was complied by his son, Mursilli II.

It has been suggested that this letter was the desperate plea of the young widow, Ankhesenamun (or possibly former Queen Meritaten), who, finding herself all alone, following the demise of her entire family, including the recent death of her husband Tutankhamun, made a final, desperate bid to either save the dynasty or to gain help in leaving Egypt to ensure her own survival and the continuation of her royal bloodline.

The tablet just describes the widow in question as 'Dakhamunzu' (the king's wife). With the rather confusing use of royal names it is difficult to pin down exactly who wrote to King Suppiluliuma I. It is possible that Meritaten was still in Egypt at this time, but equally she may already have secured help from outside Egypt and fled, perhaps inspiring her sister Ankhesenamun to also seek outside help in securing the throne?

The lady in question, who wrote this desperate letter is known only as 'Dakhamunzu', clearly not her Egyptian name, so we can only hazard an educated guess as to the true identity of the author of the letter. It is believed that 'Dakhamunzu' is a Hittite rendering of the Egyptian title 'Ta Hemet Nesu' or Pharaoh's Great Wife, but what is written on the cuneiform tablet, is only the Akkadian transliteration of the female royal title, so it is really not clear who is being referred to. This could easily be Meritaten, as she was given the title Great Royal Wife. Unfortunately we do not know the identity of the Pharaoh whose unexpected demise compelled his terrified widow to make such an extraordinary plea. In the Hittite letter, the deceased ruler is referred to only by his prenomen or throne name, so we cannot be sure of the author or the identity of her deceased husband.

We do not know the exact date of the exchange of letters but we do know that Suppiluliuma I's son Zannanza is recorded as deceased in 1324 BCE, some 10 years after Meritaten disappears from official records. Perhaps for this reason it is assumed that it was Ankhesenamun who wrote, as opposed to Meritaten, who also lost her husband and Pharaoh (Smenkhkare) some 10 years before Zannanza's death? An interesting clue is that Tutankhamun is generally regarded as dying in 1323 BCE, a year after the recorded death of Zannanza, which would imply that these events happened while Tutankhamun was still alive. If this was the case, then it could not have been Ankhesenamun who wrote to Suppiluliuma I.

"While my father was down in the country of Karchemish, he sent Lupakki and Tarkhunta(?)-zalma forth into the country of Amka. So they went to attack Amka and brought deportees, cattle and sheep back for my father. But when the people of Egypt heard of the attack on Amka, they were afraid. And since, in addition, their

Figure 24: A cuneiform tablet from 'The Deeds of Suppiluliuma', detailing events of the Zannanza Affair (held by Istanbul Archaeology Museum, photograph by Stephen Lew).

lord Nibkhururiya had died, therefore the queen of Egypt, who was Dakhamunzu, sent a messenger to my father and wrote to him thus: "My husband died. A son I have not. But to thee, they say, the sons are many. If thou wouldst give me one son of thine, he would become my husband. Never shall I pick out a servant of mine and make him my husband! ... I am afraid!" When my father heard this, he called forth the Great Ones for council (saying): "Such a thing has never happened to me in my whole life!" So it happened that my father sent forth to Egypt Hattusha-ziti, the chamberlain (with this order): "Go and bring thou the true word back to me! Maybe they deceive me! Maybe (in fact) they do have a son of their lord! Bring thou the true word back to me!"

The cuneiform tablet can currently be found in the Istanbul Archaeological Museum, Turkey. This event that unfolded from the letter became known as the 'Zannanza Affair', after Suppiluliuma's fourth son Zannanza. The events that followed were arguably a catalyst for centuries of hostility between the Egyptians and the Hittites. After some consideration Zannanza was sent to Egypt by his father but he disappeared along the way. It is speculated that he was murdered by the grand vizier Aye, who of course was the one who eventually ended up marrying Ankhesenamun (after the death of Tutankhamun) in order to become Pharaoh.

Mursilli II (son and successor of Suppiluliuma I) continues:

"But when it became spring, Hattusa-ziti [came back] from Egypt, and the messenger of Egypt, Lord Hani, came with him. Now since my father had, when he sent Hattusa-ziti to Egypt, given him orders as follows: "Maybe they have a son of their lord! Maybe

they deceive me and do not want my son for the kingship!" --
therefore the queen of Egypt wrote back to my father in a letter
thus: "Why didst thou say 'they deceive me' in that way? Had I a
son, would I have written about my own and my country's shame
to a foreign land? Thou didst not believe me and has even spoken
this to me! He who was my husband has died. A son I have not!
Never shall I take a servant of mine and make him my husband!
I have written to no other country, only to thee have I written!
They say thy sons are many: so give me one of thine! To me he
will be my husband, but in Egypt he will be king." So, my father
was kindhearted, he complied with the word of the woman and
concerned himself with the matter of a son.

My father sent foot soldiers and charioteers who attacked the
country of Amka, Egyptian territory. Again he sent troops, and
again he attacked it. When the Egyptians became frightened, they
asked outright for one of his sons to (take over) the kingship. But
when my father gave them one of his sons, they killed him as they
led him there. My father let his anger run away with him, he went
to war against Egypt and attacked Egypt..."

So, it is clear from Mursilli's account (also quoting the original
letter) that Zannanza was sent to Egypt where he was killed.
Suppiluliuma I accused the Egyptians of murdering his son,
but the new Pharaoh of Egypt, Aye II, denied the murder, but
acknowledged the death of Zannanza. Suppiluliuma was not
satisfied with the reply, which resulted in war with Egypt in the
aftermath of these events. This crisis may well have all happened
while Tutankhamun was still alive, with the outbreak of war
happening under his successor Aye II. From Hittite records we

know that Zannanza's death appears to have happened in 1324 BCE, from a few months up to almost 2 years before the death of Tutankhamun, in 1323 BCE.

Uncertain Departure

Was Meritaten the last scion of a royal family, that was now fated to collapse, perhaps after the death of her half-brother Tutankhamun? We do not know if she attempted to leave Egypt after her husband died (1334 BCE) or after her half-brother died (1323 BCE). Personally, I think she may have tried to leave after the death of her husband Smenkhkare as she is not mentioned in any records after 1334 BCE, except inside the tomb of Tutankhamun himself. Meritaten would have been aware of Tutenkhamun's fragile health, becoming Pharaoh at 8, and perhaps having no confidence that he would survive, possibly decided to try and escape Egypt. However, given that the Zannanza Affair happened before the death of Tutenkhamun, this implies that it was Meritaten who had written for help, perhaps because her brother was a powerless puppet Pharaoh, unable to protect himself or his family?

Although the name Ankhesenamun has been suggested as the true identity of the author of the letter, we know that she not only married Tutankhamun, but also maried Aye II and the final Pharaoh of the 18th dynasty - Horemheb. She was clearly a real survivor and a skilled woman, but as someone who would be aware of the great risk involved, she probably would not have written to a foreign ruler requesting help. A key fact is that her husband was still alive at the time of the Zannanza Affair and hence, I believe that it is most unlikely to have been Ankhesenamun who was the author of the letter to the Hittites.

I am, based on the weight of evidence and probabilities, convinced that it was Meritaten who wrote to the Hittite king. Some commentators have suggested that she may have written to several rulers in the locality of Egypt, but this is unproven. For someone in such a desperate situation, it would make sense for her to write more than one letter appealing for help, even if the letter did state:

"I have written to no other country, only to thee have I written!"

If she had been helped by the Hittites, she could have escaped across the Mediterranean Sea to what is now Turkey, even if that help had resulted in the death of Zannanza. However, seeing as the Hittites were generally opposed to Egypt, it would seem to many to make little sense for them to help Meritaten escape. What is clear is that there was a Hittite intervention in Egypt some time before or around 1324 BCE, that led to Zannanza's death and war between the Hittites and Egypt. We also know that, perhaps as a result of this incident that Tutankhamun was dead a year later. In addition, his Grand Visier Aye married his widow/sister Ankhesenamun and also, as Aye II, he became the new Pharaoh. The later histories, referring to Scotia, do not mention the Hittites at all. However, there are suggestions of the Phoenicians being involved, but given the passing of time and multiple sources of the story, the identities may have been confused or forgotten.

Possible Mycenaean/Phoenician Involvement

It is well known that the maritime trade routes between the Eastern and Western Mediterranean were used in the second half of the 2nd Millennium BCE by Mycenaean sailors from Greece and the Aegean Sea. This was in search of metals from western lands, especially copper, silver and tin, which were in short supply in the East. The collapse of the Mycenaean world occurred around 1200 BCE, it is believed, as a result of the invasions of the unknown and mysterious so-called 'Sea Peoples'.

This, it is speculated, led to the abandonment of these maritime routes and left the East without supplies. But undoubtedly the Phoenicians, due to their contacts with the Mycenaean world, came to know these routes and continued in the trade of metals and other goods, after the Mycenaeans disappeared from the scene. It is conceivable that a Mycenaean royal, or Mycenaean merchants helped Meritaten in her flight, but I could find no proof of any extensive links between the Mycenaeans and Egyptians, in the time frame of the Amarna Dynasty, or mention of Mycenaeans in any of the source material I researched.

The Phoenicians were notable merchants and explorers, like the Mycenaeans, who set up colonies across the Mediterranean region, due to the constant warring and difficulties in their Canaanite native areas (Lebanon and Palestine). Phoenicians was the name given to these people by the Greeks, but the Phoenicians continued to refer to themselves as Canaanites. They were allied with the Egyptians to a large extent and were eventually forced out of the northern parts of the Levant by the Hittites. Tyre was a major Phoenician seaport from about 2000 BCE through to the Roman period and it was Phoenicians from Tyre who established their colony of Carthage, as their new base (around 700 BCE). At the time of the Amarna dynasty, they would still have had control of much of the Levant, struggling to keep control of their northern areas due to the Hittites, Mitanni, Syrians and Babylonians.

To me, at least, it makes more sense that it is the Phoenicians, as opposed to distant Mycenaeans, or the Hittites, who would have been in a position to help Meritaten escape to Spain by sea. Although they were nominally favourable to Egypt and enemies of the Hittites, allegiances were continually changing throughout this time period, and indeed throughout history. Perhaps it was expedient at the time (war broke out between the Hittite and Egyptian kingdoms) or perhaps they decided to take pity on the hopeless and desperate Meritaten? Being a maritime nation, that controlled traffic and trade all across the Mediterranean, they were in a position to escort her to anywhere she wanted to go. The Hittites were not a naval power, but they did have a powerful army, whereas the Phoenicians dominated the seas in the Mediterranean, for a millennium or so. This was until the Romans challenged their power, in the Punic wars, that eventually led to their demise.

Although it cannot be proven conclusively who asked for help and if indeed help was given (with an escape), the fact that several chroniclers of Egypt and Greece, hundreds of years later, mention Scotia and her flight from Egypt, gives credibility to the story. Why would several historians make up such a story, for no reason? Given the circumstances of the Amarna period in Egypt, it is clear that later Greco-Egytian, Greek and Roman writers were almost certainly describing the flight of an Egyptian Princess or Queen of the Amarma dynasty, which happened around the time of the Zannanza Affair.

Not everyone would agree with my view on this. In his introduction to the English translation (from Latin) of John of Fordun's book, 'Chronicle of the Scottish Nation' (1360 CE),

William Skene is rather scathing of Fordun's early history of Scotland, describing it as 'fictitious':

"In constructing his scheme of the early history of Scotland, Fordun has evidently taken for its basis the genealogy deducing the kings of Scotland through a long line of Celtic ancestors from Gaedil Glass, whom he calls Gaythelos, the eponymus of the Gaelic race, which first appeared at the accession of William the Lion and again at the coronation of Alexander III. To this, as a connecting link, he adapts the later chronicles which appeared from time to time in their various forms—the earlier and more authentic documents he either was ignorant of or ignored--and endeavours to form one uniform scheme out of them; and he harmonizes this scheme with such notices as he can adapt to his purpose from the Roman writers, and such authors as Giraldus Cambrensis, Geoffrey of Monmouth, and others. In doing so, he uses to a considerable extent the same class of writers and the same kind of materials, as were employed by Higden in his Polychronicon, and very much in the same manner. And wherever he finds the word Scotia in these writers, he applies it to Scotland, and thus adopts into his history events which properly belong to Ireland, while by this process he materially aids his scheme of an early settlement of Scots in this country.

It is only when we follow in detail the manner in which he has worked out this plan that we see the great skill with which it has been done, considering the limited extent of real information he possessed, and the scanty materials at his disposal.

Beginning with Gaedil Glass, or Gaythelos, the eponymus of the race, and Scota their female ancestor, by which the country in which they settled is usually typified, he connects the names in the genealogy with a fictitious narrative of the emigration of the race from Egypt to Spain, and thence to Ireland, based to some extent upon the Irish traditions, but differing in several leading particulars from them. He then brings the Scots over from Ireland to Scotland under a leader, Ethachius Rothay, whom he finds in the genealogy several generations before Forgo or Fergus son of Feradaig- -the resemblance of the name of Rothay to that of Rothesay in the island of Bute having apparently suggested it."

In the actual text of the book, Fordun gives several versions of the story, which clearly conflict with each other, coming from different sources, at different points in history. What is apparent from this is that several historians were aware of the history or mythology of Scotia and bothered to record it in their own works, that Fordun, and later Bower, made use of. Here's a redacted extract of the story, which includes the more significant parts of the story, from chapters VI to XX (6-20):

"We gather from various writings of old chroniclers that the nation of the Scots, one of most ancient descent, sprang from the Greeks, and from the Egyptians who survived the overthrow of their fellow-countrymen and king in the Red Sea. I, therefore, think it fitting to describe the local position of the countries of Greece and Egypt, where they were fostered, as well as of the other places they traversed, and of the site of their modern habitation, so that the reader may more clearly understand in what part of the globe these are situated, and their geographical bearings."

It would appear from this that Fordun is confusing the reign of Ramsesses II with that of Akhenaten. However, given that the 'kings list' (that early histories had access to) obliterated the Amarna Pharaohs, it is not entirely surprising that the end of the 18th dynasty and the start of the 19th dynasty would be confused in the time line. Later on Fordun goes on to describe the events surrounding Scotia:

"The farthest country of Europe, on the west, is Hispania (Spain), or rather, the islands of Gades, which are in the ocean, 120 paces distant from the mainland of Spain; on these formerly Hercules fixed his pillars. There are two Hispanias, a nearer and a further, comprising the various regions of Legio, Castellum, Navarre, Arragon, and Portugal, and the provinces of Galicia, the natives of which, according to Isidore, claim a Greek origin; and Celtiberia on the river Hyber. The Scots settled in this country first, for some time. Europe comprises also many large islands, the largest of which, Albion, lies in the ocean, to the north-west. Its southern, and larger, part was formerly in-habited by the Britons, and was called Britannia, but is now known as England. Its northern portion, in like manner, being inhabited by Scots from an early period, was called Scotia; and it is now, by the help of God, the chief kingdom of the island.

The Scots possess numerous islands, a hundred or more, which have belonged to them from ancient times, and beyond the shores thereof no land is found to the north-west, except, it is said, an island called Thule, at a distance of seven days' sail from them. A day's sail beyond this, the sea is said to be sluggish and thick. Beyond Britain, also, in the ocean between it and the west, is situated the island of Ireland, where the Scots first fixed their abode."

In Chapter VIII we encounter Scotia and Gaythelos for the first time:

"In the third Age, in the days of Moses, a certain king of one of the countries of Greece, Neolus, or Heolaus, by name, had a son, beautiful in countenance, but wayward in spirit, called Gaythelos, to whom he allowed no authority in the kingdom. Roused to anger, and backed by a numerous band of youths, Gaythelos disturbed his father's kingdom by many cruel misdeeds, and angered his father and his people by his insolence. He was, therefore, driven out by force from his native land, and sailed to Egypt, where, being distinguished by courage and daring, and being of royal birth, he married Scota, the daughter of Pharaoh. Another Chronicle says that, in those days, all Egypt was overrun by the Ethiopians, who, according to their usual custom, laid waste the country from the mountains to the town of Memphis and the Great Sea; so that Gaythelos, the son of Neolus, one of Pharaoh's allies, was sent to his assistance with a large army; and the king gave him his only daughter in marriage, to seal the compact. It is written in The Legend of St. Brandan that a certain warrior, to whom the chiefs of his nation had assigned the sovereignty, reigned over Athens in Greece: and that his son, Gaythelos by name, married the daughter of Pharaoh, king of Egypt, Scota, from whom also the Scots derived their name. And he, that is, Gaythelos, who was conspicuous for strength and boldness, exasperated his father, and every one, by his waywardness, and, departing on account of the failure of his cause, rather than of his own accord, retired into Egypt, supported by a spirited band of youths. Another Chronicle, again, says: But a certain Gaythelos, the grandson, it is said, of Nembricht, being unwilling to reign by right of succession, or because the people, assisted by the neighbouring nations, would not submit to his tyranny, left his country followed by a great crowd of young men,

with an army. At length, harassed by many wars in various places, and compelled by want of provisions, he came to Egypt, and, having joined King Pharaoh, he strove, together with the Egyptians, to keep the children of Israel in perpetual bondage; and he finally married Pharaoh's only daughter, Scota, with the view of succeeding his father-in-law on the throne of Egypt."

Again we see reference to what who now regarded as Ramesses II and the flight of Moses and how Gaythelos arrived in Egypt:

"The Period at which the Scots had their Origin, and from whom; and their Outlawry from Egypt. Three thousand six hundred and eighty-nine years after the beginning of the world, in the five hundred and fifth year of the third Age, three hundred and thirty years before the taking of Troy, seven hundred and sixty years before the building of Rome, in the year 1510 B.C. (or as others put it- One thousand and five hundred years, and seventy, less one, Before the birth, as I have found, of God's incarnate Son, Was Pharaoh, following the Jews, in the Red Sea undone) the above-mentioned Pharaoh was swallowed up, with his army of 600 chariots, 50,000 horse, and 200,000 foot ; while the survivors, who remained at home, hoping to be released from the tax of grain formerly introduced by Joseph in the time of famine, suddenly drove clean out of the kingdom, with his followers, lest he should usurp dominion over them, the king's son-in-law Gaythelos Glas, who had refused to pursue the in- offensive Hebrews. Thus, then, the assembled villagers cruelly expelled from their midst, by a servile insurrection, all the nobles of the Greeks, as well as those of the Egyptians, whom the greedy sea had not swallowed up. We read in another Chronicle: After the army was gone, Gaythelos

remained behind in the city of Heliopolis, by a plan arranged between him and King Pharaoh, in case he should have to succeed him in his kingdom. But the remainder of the Egyptian people, perceiving what befell their king, and, at the same time, being on their guard lest, once subject to the yoke of a foreign tyranny, they should not be able to shake it off again, gathered together their forces, and sent word to Gaythelos that, if he did not hasten, as much as possible, his departure from the kingdom, endless mischief would result to him and his without delay."

"...he decided, to a certain extent, indeed, by the advice of his officers, that he either would seize from some other nation a kingdom and lands, and dwell there in continual warfare, or, by the favour of the gods, would only seek out some desert place to take possession of, for a settlement. This they all in concert swore to put into due execution, as far as they were able. Having, therefore, appointed Gaythelos their leader, the banished nobles, impelled to some extent by a youthful craving for adventure, soon made ready a good-sized fleet, laden with provisions in store and the other necessaries for an expedition, to go in quest of new lands to settle in, on the uttermost confines of the world, hitherto, as they imagined, unoccupied. Another Chronicle says:-Gaythelos, therefore, assembled his retainers, and, with his wife Scota, quitted Egypt; and as, on account of an old feud, he feared to retrace his steps to those parts whence he had come into Egypt, he bent his course westwards, where, he knew, the inhabitants against whom he would have to struggle with his men, un- skilled as these were in the use of arms, were fewer and less warlike."

Another Chronicle has the following account: -

"At length all was ready ; and Gaythelos, with his wife and whole family, and the other leaders, trusting to the direction of their gods, embark, in boats, on board ships prepared for them ; and when the sailors, with busy diligence, had weighed anchor, and cast off the warps, the sails are spread wide to the blasts of the winds. Then, sailing out into the inland channel, they made for the western tracts of the world, with prows cutting the waves of the sea between the southern limits of Europe and Africa."

John of Fordun goes on to describe Gaythelos making exploratory trips to Spain before settling in Spain, with his new wife, the Egyptian Princess, who he refers to as Scota. Having taken land for himself and his people by force, clearly life did not go well for them leading them to seek refuge elsewhere.

"CHAPTER XII

Stay made by Gaythelos in Africa; and cause of his first repairing to Spain.

Gaythelos then, having wandered through many provinces, and made various halts in such spots as he found convenient, because he knew that the people he led, burdened as they were with wives and children, and much baggage, were distressed beyond measure, entered Africa by the river Ansaga, and rested in quiet, for some time, in a province of Numidia, though the dwellers in that country have no habitation where they can be sure of quiet. For the forty years, therefore, that the children of Israel dwelt in the desert, under Moses, Gaythelos himself, also, with his followers, wandered, now here, now there, through many lands; but at length, leaving Africa, he embarked in such ships as he could then get, and went over into Spain, near the islands of Gades. Another Chronicle tells us:

Thus, indeed, wandering hither and thither, they kept traversing, for a long time, many unknown parts of the sea; and, forasmuch as they were driven about by the violence of contrary winds, they were exposed to many dangers, and various risks, until, at length, just as they were being pinched by want of provisions, they unexpectedly arrive safely in some part of the coast of Spain. There the ships were laid up, made fast to moorings which had been laid down."

After a long-winded explanation of why Gaythelos left Egypt, supposedly linked with Moses, he then goes on to describe them settling in Spain. Of course, Moses was not born until the 19th Dynasty period, hence all mention of him is purely to give biblical weight to the story. Such efforts to legitimize a story with biblical references were common in the Middle Ages. This extract is rather long, but her time in Spain is an important part of Scotia's story, that is often overlooked:

"CHAPTER XIII - Reason alleged by some for the Departure from Egypt of Gaythelos, and the rest who went away from the same cause. It is maintained, however, elsewhere, that many Egyptians as well as Greek foreigners, panic-stricken, not through fear of man only, as said above, but rather by dread of the gods, fled far from Egypt and their native country. Seeing the terrible plagues and wonders with which they had been afflicted, through Moses, they feared exceedingly, neither durst they remain there longer. For, as the regions of Sodom and Gomorrah, with their people, had, of old, been reduced to ashes, on account of their sins, so they expected that Egypt, with its inhabitants, would suddenly be overthrown. This is also evident from the Historia Scholastica, where it is said:-Many of the Egyptians, indeed, fearing that Egypt would be

destroyed, went forth; of whom Cecrops, crossing over into Greece, built the town of Athen, which was afterwards called Athens. It is believed, also, that Dionysian Bacchus, in that season, going forth out of Egypt, built the city of Argos, in Greece, and gave to Greece the use of the vine. Whether, indeed, she was led, in this wise, of her own accord, by fear of the gods, or forcibly compelled by her enemies (but it was certainly in one or other of these two ways), it is taught that Scota, with her husband,

followed by a large retinue, went forth in terror out of Egypt. Grosseteste says -In the olden time there went out of Egypt Scota, the daughter of Pharaoh, with her husband, by name Gayel, and a very large company. For they had heard the evils which were to come upon the Egyptians, and thus through the commands or the answers of the gods, flying from plagues which were to come, they launched out into the sea, intrusting themselves to the governance of their gods. And they, cruising thus, for many days, through the seas, with wavering minds, at length, on account of the inclement weather, were glad to bring up on a certain coast.

CHAPTER XIV - How Gaythelos obtained his first Settlement in Spain. In the meantime, being harassed by the long fatigues of the sea, they hastened to the land of Spain, for the sake of obtaining food and rest. But the natives hastily assemble from every side; and, brooking ill the arrival of the new-comers, propose to withstand them by force of arms. They are soon engaged in battle, and, after a desperate struggle, the natives are overcome and put to flight. The victory thus gained, Gaythelos pursues the natives; and, having plundered part of the surrounding country, he returned to the shore, and pitched his tents, surrounded by a mound, on a certain hillock on rising ground, where he could more safely oppose the attacking columns of the enemy. He there afterwards, the natives having been subdued for a while, built by degrees a very strong town, by name Brigancia, in the middle of which he erected a tower of exceeding height, surrounded by a deep ditch, which is still to be seen. He thus passed all the days of his life there, harassed by the continual assaults of war, and perpetually entangled in the various chances of fortune. The Legend of Saint Brandan says : -But Gaythelos, driven out of Egypt, and thus sailing through the Mediterranean Sea, brings to in Spain; and, building, on the river Hyber, a tower, Brigancia by name, he usurped by force from the inhabitants a place to settle in.

CHAPTER XV - On Account of the continual Slaughter of his People there, Gaythelos sends out Explorers to search for Lands out at Sea- Their Return when they had discovered a certain Island. Meanwhile, being there troubled by annoyances of many kinds, Gaythelos, whose whole attention was engrossed In the guardianship of his people, as became a useful and careful chief, foresaw that there was no other fate in store for him there than that he himself, with his tribe, should either be blotted out from off the face of the whole earth, or subjected to the yoke of a perpetual slavery, by the powerful tribes of Spain; for though it very often had happened that he had inflicted very great slaughter on his adversaries, he had never, however, gained even one victory without loss to his small tribe, which, far from increasing, he foresees will rather be diminished by daily and continual wasting; and thus, forecasting with watchful care, he pondered in his mind this continual slaughter, which even threatened dispersion, and what steps he should take in consequence:

and at length, debating within himself, he perceived that he deserved to suffer the difficulties he had incurred; for, inasmuch as he had renounced the design he had originally formed, on consideration, namely, to seek out unoccupied lands, without bringing injury upon any one, and had besides insulted territory held from heaven by another people, he feared that he had thus given manifold offence to his own gods. Minded, therefore, to return to the plan he had before conceived in Egypt, he, with the advice of his council, calls the seamen together, and straightway directs them, being provided with arms, and boats provisioned with victuals, to explore the boundless ocean, in search of some desert land. They duly put off to the ships, set sail, and leave the coast of Spain; and, leaving behind them the places they knew, enter an unknown sea. After a most speedy passage, by the favour of the gods, they perceive, looming up afar off, an island washed by the sea on all sides; and having reached it, and put into the nearest harbour, they make the circuit of the island, to explore it. When they had examined it as thoroughly as they could, they row quickly back to Brigancia, bringing their King Gaythelos tidings of a certain most beautiful tract of land, discovered in the ocean."

So, we see in this version of the story (Fordun) that Gaythelos and his wife Scota leave Egypt and decide to leave for Spain, where they founded Brigancia, but after a disastrous sojourn in Spain, they left for an island further west, discovered by some of Gaythelos' men. Their intention was to leave Spain to go and settle in this newly discovered western Island. In Walter Bower's version of the story, Gaythelos is also called 'Goídel Glas', his work is thought to be mainly based on Manetho's account of Gaythelos and Scotia, although he was clearly familiar with Fordun's work too.

Gaythelos was apparently a Greek prince, forced into exile by his father. He sailed south to Egypt where the Pharaoh Chencres was in a struggle to drive the Ethiopians out of his lands and back to their southern kingdom. At various times they had ruled parts of Egypt, note that the area known then as Ethiopia is not the same geographically as the modern day country. Gaythelos joined his army with that of the Pharaoh, so that together they pushed the Ethiopians out, according to the story. Gaythelos formed another alliance with Chencres to help keep the Israelites in bondage and so in recognition of Gaythelos' assistance and loyalty, Chencres gave his daughter Scota in marriage to Gaythelos. Of course we can only guess the actual names of the characters involved, as none of them exist in any recorded histories of the region.

Bower's 'Scotichronicon' tells us that Chencres was the Pharaoh who died when the Red Sea parted, as he was chasing the Israelites, who is generally regarded as Ramesses II today. The people of Egypt, were looking for reform and saw the death of the Pharaoh as an opportunity for change and thus Gaythelos (a continuation of the status quo) was driven into exile. While the details are vague, this description would fit well with the dissatisfied people of Egypt under Akhenaten, some hundred or less years before Ramesses II reigned. It is quite possible that Bower's book conflates several different versions of real events in the Amarna period (circa 1351-1320 BCE) with the reign of Ramesses II (1279–1213 BCE). There is a gap of some 40-90 years and different dynasties, but to Bower, writing some 2500 years later, this would all be lost on him, without a doubt.

The entourage that went into exile with Gaythelos proclaimed him king and called themselves 'Scots'" after their queen Scota or Scotia, but these rulers and their subjects lacked a kingdom. They wandered the desert for years before Gaythelos took his people from the African continent to the Iberian Peninsula (Spain). It is here that they settled in the northwest corner of the peninsula, at a place called Brigancia. The Romans later called this city 'Brigantium' and it is now the city of A Coruña, located at the north-west tip of the autonomous province of Galicia, Spain.

The following extract, from Walter Bower's 'Scotichronicon', describes the flight from Egypt to Spain :

"Book I - The Legend of Gaythelos and Scota

Bower (following Fordun) cites many variants of the foundation legend of the Scottish kingdom. The following selection of extracts threads its way through the main story. Pharaoh Chencres cannot now be identified. Brigantia is the modern Corunna in north-west Spain (i.e., not in fact on the river Ebro, but looking north to Ireland). The explanation of the division between Gaels and Scots comes from Gerald of Wales, Topographia Hibernica.

From various writings of ancient chroniclers, we deduce that the nation of the Scots is of ancient stock, taking its first beginning from the Greeks and those of the Egyptians who were left after the rest of them had been drowned in the Red Sea along with their king. In the third age in the time of Moses, there was a certain king of one of the kingdoms of Greece called Neolus or Eolaus. He had a son who was good looking but mentally unstable, Gaythelos by name. Since he had not been permitted to hold any position of power in the kingdom, he was provoked to anger, and with the support of a large company of young men he inflicted many disasters on his father's kingdom with frightful cruelty. He greatly outraged both his father and the inhabitants [of the country] with his violent behaviour. So he was driven out of his native land and sailed off to Egypt; and there, since he was outstandingly brave and daring and also of royal descent, he was united in marriage with Scota, the daughter of the Pharaoh Chencres.

The aforesaid Pharaoh was drowned with his armies including 600 chariots, 50,000 cavalry and 200,000 infantry. Now those who survived by staying at home, hoping to be freed from the servitude of the corn-tax formerly imposed by Joseph in time of famine, unexpectedly drove the king's son-in-law Gaythelos Glas (who wished to pursue the innocent Hebrews) right out of the kingdom along with his followers for fear that he might establish dominion over them. So all the nobles, both Greek and Egyptian alike, whom the voracious sea had failed to devour were cruelly driven away by peasants enrolled in a servile uprising.

So Gaythelos gathered together all his followers and left Egypt with his wife Scota. Because he was afraid to return to the regions from which he had come to Egypt because of old feuds, he directed his course westwards, where he knew there were fewer and less warlike peoples with whom he would have to fight, since the men there were untrained in fighting.

The legend of St. Brendan: "Now Gaythelos was driven from Egypt and after sailing in this way over the Mediterranean Sea he landed in Spain. He built a tower on the River Ebro, having seized by force from the inhabitants a place for his settlement called Brigantia. There his descendants multiplied greatly... He summoned his sailors and ordered them to take arms, to provision small ships with all speed and to explore the boundless Ocean in search of uninhabited lands. They went off to their ships, unfurled their sails and left the Spanish shore. Leaving behind the known, they made for unknown regions over the sea. After sailing with good speed and guided by the favour of the gods, they saw an island rising up in the distance surrounded on all sides by salt sea. They put into a nearby harbour on this island and, after beaching their ships, went all round exploring the island. After seeing as much of the island as they could, they sailed quickly back to Brigantia, reporting to their king Gaythelos on the very beautiful tract of land that they had found in Ocean.

CHAPTER XVI - (Same continued) He exhorts his Sons to go to that Island.

Now Gaythelos, since he was unacceptable to the inhabitants, looking forth, one clear day, from Brigancia, and seeing land far out at sea, arms some active and warlike youths, and directs them to explore it in three boats; and they commit themselves to the high seas. They, at length, against a northerly wind, came in a body to the island, and, rowing round it to re-connoitre, attacked the inhabitants they found, and slew them. And, thus, having explored the land, and admired its goodliness, they return to Brigancia. But Gaythelos, overtaken by sudden death, exhorted his sons, and impressed upon them that they should do their best to get possession of the aforesaid land, charging them with both slothfulness and cowardice if they gave up so noble a kingdom, and one which they could penetrate into without war or danger. Whatever happen to me," said he, you will be able, they say, to make this island your habitation. When we, driven by want of food, arrived in this country, our gods gave us the victory over the opposing inhabitants; and justly so, had we, as soon as our ships had been provisioned, set sail and gone to this island, which the gods now offer us, or to one, like it, devoid of inhabitants."

While these accounts are very interesting to read, they are considered by many academics to be historically almost worthless, as they are constructed from various confused earlier accounts, with loss of the original names of those involved, or confusion with similar characters from another time. Add to this that there probably was a fair amount of embellishment and speculation thrown in, it does not lend credibility to these 'pseudo-histories' in terms of accuracy. However, this does not mean that the entire story is invalid, it is unlikely that all of Fordun's and Bower's stories are fabrications, they are most likely based on actual events, but the stories have become horribly mutated and distorted, to the point that they have lost much of their validity as historical documents.

So one must ask, is there actually any real evidence of Meritaten, or any Egyptian royals, living in Spain? Who was Gaythelos, or Goídel Glas and where did he come from? Was there ever a settlement called Brigancia or Brigantium? If this place existed is A Coruña, in Galicia, actually the same location that Gaythelos and Scotia once lived?

During the research for this book, the trail initially ran cold at Spain, but after some considerable digging I was able to find quite some evidence of Egyptian activity in Spain, in the ancient past. My search began with A Coruña, which is the location of the world's oldest standing lighthouse.

A Coruña/Brigantium

The light house at A Coruña is known as The Tower of Hercules, which was not built by the Greeks, but by the Romans in the 1st century CE. So this structure was created some 1300 years after the events we are concerned with, but at a place once called Brigantium or Brigancia, as mentioned in the Scottish accounts. In fact the lighthouse was formerly known as the Farum Brigantium until the 20th century. The nearby town of Betanzos also lays claim to the ancient name Brigantia/Britantium, but having a much smaller harbour and no importance as a Roman site, it is highly unlikely to be the case. Various Greek, Roman and Celtic myths exist around the origins of the lighthouse, but curiously such a building is mentioned in the Irish account 'Lebor Gabála Érenn' (the Book of Invasions).

Supporting evidence for more ancient towers comes from a site much further inland in central Spain - La Peñuela. It is in this region that we find the Motilla, an ancient settlement, particularly of the La Mancha region. These motillas or hillforts are from the Early-Middle Bronze Age, starting around 2200 BCE and falling into disuse around 1200 BCE, with this copper-rich region having trade connections across the Mediterranean. The Motilla included central towers of up to 5m in height. While this is hardly impressive compared to the Farum Brigantium, it shows the ability to build stone towers of a significant height.

The excavations of one such Motilla in 1947 at La Peñuela yielded amazing finds at the base of the main tower - bronze daggers and arrowheads. Analysis of these weapons by Dr Joaquin Jimenez showed they were Bronze Age, dated to approximately 1340 BCE.

So, the idea of the people of ancient Spain constructing a large tower, as described by the Scottish and Irish texts, does not seem so far-fetched after all. In the story (from The Book of Invasions) king Breogán, who is given as the founding father of the Galician Celts, constructed a huge tower that was so tall that

Figure 25: The Roman lighthouse of Brigantium (the Tower of Hercules) at A Coruña at the north-west tip Spain. In the foreground is a modern statue of the legendary king Breogán (Photograph by Luis Miguel Bugallo Sánchez).

one of his sons (Íth) could see a distant green shore from its top. That glimpse of a distant green land lured them to sail north to Ireland. According to the legends, Breogán's descendants invaded and settled in Ireland and are the Celtic ancestors (the Gaels) of the current people of Ireland. In the modern era, a huge statue of Breogán was erected at the entrance to the walkway that leads to the lighthouse at A Coruña. Below is the relevant extract from 'Lebor Gabála Érenn':

"SECTION VIII. – THE SONS OF MÍL

The Taking Of The Gáedil

The taking of the Gáedil and their synchronizing, here below. As for the Gáedil, we have given their adventures from Iafeth s. Noe onward, and from the Tower of Nemrod, till we have left them at Breogan's Tower in Spain; and how they came from Egypt, and out of Scythia to the Maeotic Marshes, and along the Tyrrhene Sea to Crete and to Sicily; and we have further related how they took Spain by force. We shall now tell you below simply how they came to Ireland.

Íth s. Breogan, [it is he] who saw Ireland at the first, on a winter's evening, from the top of Breogan's Tower; for thus is a man's vision best, on a clear winter's evening. Íth, with thrice thirty warriors, came to Ireland, and they landed on the "Fetid Shore" of the Headland of Corcu Duibne, what time they arrived

As for Íth s. Breogan, it was he who found Ireland at the first. He came alone, on a clear winter's evening, on to the top of Breogan's Tower, and he began to spy out the sea far to the north-east, till he saw Ireland away from him. He goes round back thereafter to his other brethren, and tells them what he had seen. Brego s. Breogan said that what he had seen was no land at all, but a cloud of the sky, and he was for hindering him from going thither; but Íth he could in no wise hinder. [Íth] launched his ship on the sea and sailed to Ireland, with thrice fifty warriors; till they landed in the "Fetid Shore" of Mag Ítha, on the Northern side of Ireland."

So, we can immediately see a link between the settlement of Gaythelos and Scotia, their mythical Brigancia/Brigantia and the ancient city of Brigantium, which has now become known as A Coruña.

According to The Legend of Brendan (recounted by Bower), Gaythelos died suddenly, but before doing so, he urged his sons to leave Spain and invade this new land with an army. Presumably on his deathbed, he accused them of laziness and cowardice if they gave up such a notable opportunity, even considering the dangers and the risks of failure. This account in 'Lebor Gabála Érenn' is very similar to the details given in Chapter 16 of the 'Scotichronicon' by Bower (earlier in this chapter).

"One of the sons of Gaythelos called Hiber, young in years but strong of purpose, was roused to war and took up arms. He got ready an expedition as best he could and approached the aforesaid island. He killed some of the few inhabitants whom he found and enslaved the rest, but he claimed the whole land as a possession for himself and his brothers, calling it Scotia after his mother's name."

The 'Lebor Gabála Érenn' goes on to describe the death of Íth in Ireland and the return of his body to Spain:

"It is then that a plot was laid by them (the Irish Tuatha Dé Danann) to kill Íth, and they bade him begone out of Ireland; and he came away from them, from Ailech to Mag Ítha. There was a pursuit after

him as far as that, and he fell in the hands at Mag Ítha: unde Mag Ítha nominatur, So it was to avenge Íth that the sons of Míl [to wit, the Gáedil] came for his [Íith's] body was carried to Spain."

The Irish text does not say where in Spain he was brought to, but we can presume that it was Brigantia, as mentioned by Bower, which is, by all indications, the location of 'Breogan's Tower in Spain', mentioned in 'Lebor Gabála Érenn'.

So, unreliable as they are, the ancient 'pseudo-histories' of Ireland, Scotland and folklore accounts in Spain offer probably some grain of truth amongst all the distortions, corruptions and confusions. Not everyone would agree with me, but I am of the opinion that they are a very muddled and confused account of actual events that took place some 3300 plus years ago, although the accounts seem to disagree on the time period and the names of people involved.

Having investigated the work of Ramón Sainero, Professor at UNED (Madrid), and Director of the Institute of Celtic Studies (IEC) it appears he has much to say on the subject of Breogán. He has also spent much of his career researching 'Lebor Gabála Érenn' in the context of Spain. The main thrust of his work may demonstrate how many of the historical events describing ancient 'pseudo-histories' such as this, were not pure invention. At least in part, the accounts provide a historical and literary interpretation which are much more truthful than has previously been considered. However, he states that there are no major Spanish works that describe these events, much of what is known is in local legends or from Irish monks who brought the story to Spain.

This brings me now to actual evidence that might corroborate the presence of Egyptians in ancient Spain. If there is no evidence of the Egyptians having ever visited Spain then this would not help in corroborating the possibility of Meritaten (Scotia) having spent a number of years living there, presumably with some form of Egyptian entourage and also the forces of her rescuer.

Physical Evidence of Egyptian Contact with Spain

In 1963, with the discovery and excavation of the Phoenician necropolis of the Sexi colony in Almuñécar (Granada, Spain), new evidence was found which was quite ground breaking. Amongst other finds, an extraordinary set of large Egyptian alabaster vases were discovered, reused in the necropolis as cinerary urns. Some of these vases bore hieroglyphic inscriptions, among which some cartouches bore the names of the Pharaohs Osorcon II, Tacelotis II and Sesonquis III stood out, all of them belonging to the 22nd Dynasty. While this is much later than the Amarna period, it was an unexpected example of early contact between Iberia and the Egyptians.

It is thought that the Phoenician oldest colonial settlement was Gadir (modern Cadiz), an establishment necessary to ensure trade and most probably founded around 1100 BCE. Hence, according to the hypothesis of Professor Josep Padró the silver from the Tanis necropolis (Psusennes I, 1039-991 BCE, 21st Dynasty) most likely would have come from the Iberian Peninsula and was taken to Egypt by Phoenician sailors, probably from Tyre. Once again, this is much later than the Amarna period, but it does demonstrate the strong likelihood of trade between Iberia and Egypt.

The 2021 excavation of the San Vicente Hill in Salamanca, central northern Spain, some 300km south east of ancient Brigantium (modern A Coruña) unearthed amulets of the Egyptian goddess Hathor, made in ancient Egypt and are thought to have reached the Iberian peninsula around 1000 BCE. It seems that Salamanca also appears in the trade routes for minerals such as iron or tin and was an important city at that time. Although this find is from approximately 300 years after the events of the Amarna period, it does demonstrate that Egyptian goods, and possibly Egyptian people were to be found in Spain in the ancient world.

According to official sources, the Egyptians did not have any colonies outside of the Middle East and there is no direct evidence that I have found to prove otherwise. What can be proven is that there were foreign colonies in ancient Spain. One colony was of the Tartessian culture, which became prominent from the 9th century BCE onwards before vanishing completely about 500 years later. This region, in south-west Spain, known as Tartessos, was fabled for its gold and the wealth of the area and its people.

The second colony of interest is that of the Phoenicians, which ran across most of the southern coast of Spain. The oldest finds in connection with the Phoenicians in Spain were made in the area of the modern port of Huelva, which was once the ancient city of Onoba. This city is within the area once known as Tartessos. It was here that archaeologists discovered the remains of a rubbish pit of a Phoenician trading post that was in use permanently during the 10th century BCE.

Again this is much later than the events of the Amarna period, but we do know for certain that the Phoenicians were in contact with Egypt during the Amarna period from mentions in the Amarna letters. For instance, the ancient Phoenician city of Arqa (in modern Lebanon), which was founded during the Early Bronze Age IV (after 3300 BCE). During the Amarna period Phoenicia was well established with trade routes reputedly reaching beyond the Pillars of Hercules (the end of the Mediterranean Sea) and as far east as Afghanistan.

Trade as far away as Britain was actually common, far more than one might think, in the 2nd millennium BCE. Research from Cambridge University shows that around 1700 BCE there was a sudden glut of British copper for export, with the discovery of the exceptionally rich copper ores of the Great Orme mine. This mine, on the north Wales coast, turned out to be one of the largest Bronze Age copper mines in Europe. Probably in response to the sheer richness and easily-worked nature of the Great Orme ores, all the other copper mines in Britain had closed by 1600 BCE. The Great Orme mine met an increasing demand for metalwork of all types (axes, spearheads, rapiers), which it satisfied for around 200 years.

Not only this, the exceptionally rich British tin deposits found in Cornwall and Devon were also vitally important in enabling the complete changeover from copper to bronze (10% tin, 90% copper), which occurred not only in Britain (circa 2100 BCE) but also across all of Europe and the Middle East, where tin is very scarce. While some tin was exported from Asia into the Mediterranean region, much of the copper was coming from Britain and Ireland, and tin in particular was coming from Britain throughout the Bronze Age. There is certainly evidence of tin ingots from Great Orme mine being used as far afield as modern Israel (which borders modern Egypt).

In addition to the ancient trade in tin, there is strong evidence of ancient trade in Amber, as discussed in detail by Lorraine Evans, in her book 'Kingdom of the Ark'. From her own research and referring to Rice (Amber - the Golden Gem of the Ages), she argues that this trade was as early as around 3000 BCE. Certainly the Egyptians were using Baltic (Scandinavian and Russian) amber by the 7th century BCE, but there is evidence of trade with the Southern Europeans and Myceneans as far back as 1800 BCE possibly. As early as 1885, German scientist Otto Helm proved that Mycenean amber finds had originated in the Baltic region.

Further evidence of early Amber trade was discovered by Dr J Oppert, in 1876, when he translated an Assyrian cuneiform inscription that was written on an obelisk that had been found at the ancient city of Ninevah (in south-east Iraq), dating to around 2000 BCE. The inscription read:

"In the sea of changeable winds
His merchants fished for pearls
In the sea where the North Star culminates
They fish for yellow amber."

While this short text does not specify where the amber came from, it is clearly somewhere to the north. The writer could have been referring to possibly the Baltic Sea or possibly the Black Sea. It is impossible to be sure about this, but what is clear is that there was trade in Amber in Mesopotamia at this time, which is further away on land from the Baltic than Egypt is. As with metals, amber is easily transportable and in this time period, travel by sea was faster and safer than across land through many kingdoms, some of which may have been hostile. It seems to me to be unthinkable that ancient civilisations did not use long-distance shipping for trade during the Amarna period and long before that even.

If the people who rescued Meritaten (Scotia) were sea-faring folk (called Armenians in 'Lebor Gabála Érenn') they could well have been Mitannian, Mycenean, Hittite or Phoenician people. Given that we lack specific details, it is completely unclear which ethnic/cultural group is concerned here, but given the extent of travel (Spain and later Scotland and Ireland) and the wide ranging trade network of the Phoenicians - it seems most likely that the people accompanying her were Phoenicians.

While there is clear indication of Egyptian artefacts as early as 1000 BCE in Iberia (Spain) and Phoenician contact as early as 900 BCE, this does not really prove anything in relation to the flight of Meritaten from Egypt. We do know that international trade between Britain and the eastern Mediterranean was happening after 1700 BCE, but this is not particularly helpful in tracing Meritaten in Spain.

However, some surprising evidence regarding Egypt did come to light concerning the controversial work of Spanish archaeologist Buenaventura Hernández Sanahuja (1810 - 1891 CE), in an article which is translated (by Google) from the Spanish original:

"Nearly two centuries ago, on 9 March 1850, Buenaventura Hernandez Sanahuja discovered in the area of the quarry of the Port of Tarragona, where today stands the Exhibition Hall of the city, parts of an Egyptian tomb. Five years later, not far from there was discovered an Egyptian mummy.

The fragments of the tomb are now at the Royal Academy of History in Madrid, and were exhibited at the Museum of the city of Tarragona to mark the centenary of the death of the archaeologist B. Hernandez Sanahuja in 1891.

In the Museum of Tarragona are exhibited three Egyptian scarabs and the piece of a brass sphinx. There is no clear chronology. The whereabouts of the mummy as to where the mummy was found are unknown. The official view is that this is a scam, but there is data in books from the last century about it.

The story of the discovery of these unique remains is the following, as Hernandez Sanahuja explains himself in his work (1855):

Summary historical-critical of the city of Tarragona, from its establishment to the Roman period, with an explanation of fragments of Egyptian tomb discovered in March 1850:

In March 1850, prison-workers assigned to the port quarry, found at the site of the Protestant cemetery a pavement of large slabs belonging to the Roman period. Deeper down they found what was, by all indications, another layer of Greek-Iberian origin. Between the Greek-Iberian layer and the bed rock, they found the controversial Egyptian shrine, covered with red inlay... Unfortunately, the workers destroyed the monument, believing that it was of no interest."

Hernandez Sanahuja's work was not well received at the time as it challenged the established view about contact with Egypt. However, an old Spanish manuscript details exactly such a thing: Los cinco libros primeros dela Coronica general de España, que recopilaua el maestro Florian de Ocampo, en casa de Iuan Iñiguez de Lequericam 1578 CE. This Catalan 'pseudo-history' states that Tarragona was named for Tarraho, eldest son of the bibilcal Tubal circa 2407 BCE; another account (derived from the Roman Strabo and Greek Megasthenes) attributes the name to 'Tearcon the Ethiopian', who is thought to be Taharqa an early 7th BCE Pharaoh of the 25th dynasty, who campaigned in Spain.

"Sanahuja, in the work cited, gives a lengthy description of 40 of the fragments that were saved from the quarry and other related finds discovered two years later. Carles Babot Boixeda, the Deputy Mayor of Tarragona Heritage in early last century transcribed the manuscript of Buenaventura Hernandez Sanahuja ("Fifteen years postscript"). Concerning the controversial remains of the Egyptian tomb and its affiliates there was expressed new currents of archaeological and anthropological studies of the time. These opinions "retreated" from their earlier statements first and revised the previous opinions. The Berlin Academy, among others, had carefully studied the remains and described them as "Apocrypha", i.e. a more or less successful Recreation probably made in the early Christian era by artists who wanted to emulate an Egyptian-style tomb. He explains that the main reason the Berlin Academy rejected the idea of the presence of any Egyptian colony in Spain was the lack of Egyptian records regarding such a colony."

The article goes on to describe how Hernandez Sanahuja felt obliged to withdraw his original opinions on the finds, in order to save his reputation.

"The manuscript goes on to explain that effectively, says Mr. Ross.... these monuments are of fictitious or doubtful provenance. They belong to an indeterminate period, depict abnormal or whimsical

representations lending themselves to various interpretations, such as are not rare in Europe…we know of other findings similar to those of Tarragona, discovered in Sardinia in the fifteenth century, about which the distinguished Italian archaeologist, General Alberto of Marmara wrote a scholarly essay in 1853… After making a brief description of the different opinions of various researchers on the fragments Sanahuja tells us that: "…All these considerations prompted us to remove the background booklet about the grave and not mention it as historical fact.

He gives no account here, however, concerning the constant pressure he had to suffer from certain sectors that led him at one stage to get rid of some of the findings…the possibility was raised on many occasions, along with threats and insinuations, that he lose his official position because of the much discussed archaeological discovery, - I refer here to the fact that many archaeologists and researchers have had to suffer and endure similar treatment in our time…"

Furthermore "Los Bere" by Spanish author Alexandre Eleazar presents an unconventional interpretation of ancient history, diverging significantly from established historical narratives. He claims that the ancient Greeks did not establish cities in the Iberian Peninsula, Italy, or France. Stating that the most significant ancient civilization was the "Empire of the Paios", which founded many important cities across Europe and the Near East.

Eleazar emphasizes the importance of linguistic analysis and the deciphering of ancient scripts, which he believes hold the true keys to understanding history. He claims to have successfully translated numerous ancient texts, including ancient Iberian and Etruscan, which are generally regarded as untranslatable lost languages. Using the Iberian texts, translated into a language very similar to current Euskera [Basque], he states:

"...something more than five thousand Egyptian troops arrived in the Iberian Peninsula to conduct a military campaign and occupy those territories."

Elsewhere in his book Eleazar states that the Catalan (north-west Spain) area that swept to one side and the other from the mouth of the Ebro River, and that is now the modern city of Tortosa, was founded by an Egyptian Pharaoh and his troops:

"The pharaoh TEO II ....founded the city of Tarteose and appointed an Egyptian prince over Iberia."

However the only reference to a Pharaoh of that or a similar name is Teos, from the 30th dynasty, who ruled briefly circa 360–358 BCE. He did conduct military campaigns into Palestine and Phoenicia and perhaps other territories controlled by the Persians. After a rebellion in Egypt Taos fled but was returned (by Persian king Artaxerxes II) in chains to the new Egyptian Pharaoh. If this is true, it would still be some 1000+ years after the Amarna period.

Eleazar also states that the much sought Tartessos Kingdom (the ancient world's version of El Dorado) in the south-west of the Iberian Peninsula (which I mentioned earlier) was actually Egyptian. This civilization is known to have begun at least as early as 1000 BCE, but none of the established archaeology seems to indicate an Egyptian origin.

Excavations of human remains at a site in Badajoz (led by Victoria Peña, from the University of Madrid) is providing unprecedented insights into Tartessian civilization, where teeth and the bones which have been removed for further study will be subjected to DNA analysis. The DNA can also tell us about the origins of these people and if they are related to the present-day inhabitants of Badajoz Province or to another group of people - such as the ancient Egyptians.

Alexandre Eleazar's opinions and writing is somewhat controversial, as there is no record of such an empire, and no other versions of his 'Iberian translations' are published, but I would be inclined to agree with him on this - that many cities attributed to the Greeks were perhaps founded much earlier, by the Phoenicians or Egyptians. Tarragona is in north-west Spain, very far away from ancient Brigantia, mentioned in the Irish texts. However it does seem to set a precedent as regards an Egyptian colony on Spanish soil in the ancient past.

Much as the plethora of finds in Spain, with regard to Egypt have largely been dismissed, the original excavators of Carthage (in Tunisia) Icat and Guielly stated in 1892 of the Iberian Peninsula (opposite Carthage) that:

"The extreme antiquity of the findings belongs to such a distant era that could be attributed to an Egyptian colony."

While it is not fashionable to consider that the Egyptians did anything more than trade with the ancient Iberians, there is certainly a large body of evidence to the contrary, but it is mostly forgotten about or withheld from the public arena.

In conclusion, there is no firm physical evidence of Meritaten escaping from Egypt to Spain. We do know that she disappeared from the Egyptian records, and that an Egyptian royal woman (who is most likely her) appealed to the Hittite king for assistance. There are no verifiable records of Meritaten (Scotia) leaving Egypt, but there is also no record of her death, her tomb was left unused in Amarna and no other tomb has been found belonging to her, or a corpse/mummy that can be attributed to her.

The legendary or 'pseudo-history' accounts do indicate that she spent some time in Spain but that she did not reside there permanently. The Spanish sources and archeology also are indicative of Egyptian influence and possible colonisation within the ancient Iberian peninsula, however this is a region that was in later times invaded by Celtic Tribes, Greeks, Romans, Phoenicians, the Huns and eventually the Moors. The archaeological evidence does give a clear picture of Egyptian contact in the early 1st millennium BCE, but it is quite possible, and even likely, that this may have occurred much earlier, due to international trade networks that were established fairly early on in the 2nd millennium BCE.

ARRIVAL IN SCOTLAND

There is no exact evidence, acceptable to historians or archaeologists, of Meritaten/Scotia having ever been in Scotland, but there is strong evidence of Egyptians having arrived in north-eastern Britain at around the time that Meritaten disappeared from Egypt. The Scotia story is backed-up to an extent, at least as a possibility, by the wrecks of two Egyptian ships, discovered near Hull in 1937 CE. Hull is slightly inland, on the north-east coast of England, in what was once the southern tip of the kingdom of Northumbria (referred to by the Romans as Maximus Caesarienus or Britannia Maxima). Northumbria included a large part of what is now modern-day Scotland. The wrecked Egyptian ships have been radio-carbon-dated to the period around 1350 BCE, which, is only 15 years off from the date given for the death of Pharaoh Smenkhkare. Given the margin for era in dating can be quite large, this very possibly was the flotilla that Scotia/Meritaten arrived in. It might also imply that the Egyptians had already had contact with Britain some time before the disappearance of Meritaten.

Unreliable as they may be, we must rely on the ancient 'pseudo-histories' for information of what may have happened. Mention of her arrival in Scotland comes from John of Fordun's 'Chronicle of Scotland' (Chronica Gentis Scotorum):

"CHAPTER XVI

Same continued He exhorts his Sons to go to that Island. Now Gaythelos, since he was unacceptable to the inhabitants, looking forth, one clear day, from Brigancia, and seeing land far out at sea, arms some active and warlike youths, and directs them to explore it in three boats; and they commit themselves to the high seas. They, at length, against a northerly wind, came in a body to the island, and, rowing round it to reconnoitre, attacked the inhabitants they found, and slew them. And, thus, having explored the land, and admired its goodliness, they return to Brigancia. But Gaythelos, overtaken by sudden death, exhorted his sons, and impressed upon them that they should do their best to get possession of the afore-said land, charging them with both slothfulness and cowardice if they gave up so noble a kingdom, and one which they could penetrate into without war or danger. Whatever happen to me," said he, you will be able, they say, to make this island your habitation. When we, driven by want of food, arrived in this country, our gods gave us the victory over the opposing inhabitants; and justly so, had we, as soon as our ships had been provisioned, set sail and gone to this island, which the gods now offer us, or to one, like it, devoid of inhabitants."

Walter Bower's history of Scotland traces the origin of the Scottish people back to Gaythelos and his progeny with Scotia. He describes the coronation of Alexander III (crowned 1249 CE) and the genealogical recital given at that event by an elderly Scotsman, in a long-held tradition:

"Europe also has many large islands, the largest of which is Albion situated in Ocean in the north-west. Its southern and larger part was once inhabited by Britons and called Britannia, but its name now is England. The northern part was inhabited from antiquity by the Scots and was called Scotland, which at the present time also is a kingdom ruled by its own prince under the protection of God. The Scots also have many islands to the number of one

hundred or more in their possession from ancient times. Beyond their shores in the north-west, there is no land to be found except for a certain island, so men say, called Thule seven days' sailing time away from them. One day's sailing time beyond that, they say, the sea is motionless and solid...

There are also other islands in an arm of a sea of Ocean which is called the Firth of Forth, namely Bass, Fidra, May, where the priory is a cell of the canons of St. Andrew of Kilrymont, and where St. Adrian is buried with his companions, the hundred holy martyrs. There is another island twelve miles from there which is called Inchkeith, on which St. Adomnan formerly ruled as abbot. He received St. Servanus and his companions with honour on that island at his first arrival in Scotland. There is a third island as well towards...

Bending his knee in a scrupulously correct manner and incliing his head, he greeted the king in his mother tongue, saying courteously: 'God bless the king of Albany, Alexandewr Mac Alexander, Mac William, Mac Henry, Mac David.'

Then this same Scot read right through the aforesaid genealogy, linking up each person with the next, until he came to the first Scot, that is Hiber the Scot. This Iber was the son of Gaythelos, the son of Neolus, formerly king of the Athenians by Scota daughter of the king of Egypt the Pharaoh Chencrees.

So, the Scots gain additional lustre from the fact that they are sprung from the stock of the kings of Athens, the chief city and capital of the Greeks. It was from there, as our sources tell us, that Greece, with its provinces, became an imperial power, a nursery of great soldiers and mother of philosophy, and invented and fostered all the beneficial branches of learning."

Bower, in Book 1 of his 'Scotichronicon' states:

"In the book of the miracles of Ireland I have found it written as follows - that the Hibernians are also called Gaitheli and Scoti.

'As ancient histories record... Gaythelos the grandson of Phenius became highly skilled in a variety of languages. Because of his skill the king Pharaoh gave him his daughter and heir Scota as his wife. So since the Hibernians are originally descended from Gaythelos and Scota, they are named Gaitheli [Gaels] and Scoti [Scots] according to their birth. Gaythelos, so they say, invented the Hibernian language which is also called Gaelic, that is to say compiled from all the languages.'

The reason for what was once upon a time called Albany now being called Scotia is found in the same passage: 'The northern part of the island of Britain is called Scotia because this land is known to have been inhabited by a people originally descended from the Scoti. This is demonstrated by the affinity of both language and culture, of arms and customs right up to the present day.'"

It is well attested that the Irish language (Gaeilge) is the mother of the Scottish language (Gàidhlig), also known as Scots/Scottish Gaelic, which developed from Old Irish. It became a distinct language some time in the 13th century, but even today some 90% of words are the same or similar between the two languages.

A Gaeilgeoir (Irish speaker) and a Scots speaker can understand each other fairly well to this day, even though there are some differences in the spelling of words and pronunciation. In Scotland it is known that ancient names for Scotland are

Albany, Albion and Alba, and in Ireland Scotland was often referred to as Alba. Interestingly enough the modern Irish word for Scotland is Albain, confirming what Bower stated well over 500 years ago.

Both Fordun and Bower mention the arrival of the Scots from Ireland, having departed from Scotland, Gaythelos and Scota became the progenitors of the Gaelic tribe the Scoti and it is their descendants that returned to Scotland. However, I am getting ahead of myself here, and we must discuss the arrival in Ireland, before returning to the subject of the descendants of Scotia/Scotia.

There is further mention of the origin of the Gaels in 'Lebor Gabála Erenn' (The Book of the Taking of Ireland):

"Now that is the time when Gaedel Glas, [from whom are the Gaedil] was born, of Scota d. Pharao. From her are the Scots named, ut dictum est Feni are named from Feinius a meaning without secretiveness: Gaedil from comely Gaedel Glas, Scots from Scota."

And again, with Nel being equated with Míl/Milesius:

"After Feinius, the hero of ocean, there was great envy
between the brethren: Nel slew Nenual, who was not gentle;
the High King was expelled.

He went into Egypt through valour till he reached powerful
Pharao; till he bestowed Scota, of no scanty beauty, the
modest, nimble daughter of pharao.

Scota bore a son to noble Nel, from whom was born a perfect
great race: Gaedel Glas was the name of the man -green were
his arms and his vesture."

Figure 26: A page from the Scotchichronicon, abridged by the author Walter Bower around 1450 CE. This particular manuscript belonged to the Abbey of Coupar Angus (held in the Advocates' Library, Edinburgh. Public domain photograph).

DNA Evidence of the Stories

There are many similarities between the different versions described in the ancient accounts, the most obvious one being the voyage from Iberia (Spain) to Ireland. In recent years, there have been significant advances in the science of DNA, which has enabled scholars to look at the ancient myths in a different context and lend them credibility in some cases. One scientist in this area, Dr. Bryan Sykes, has specialised in the study of DNA and applied it to the history of humanity.

Dr. Sykes, Professor of Human Genetics at Oxford University, has utilised his laboratory to explore the genetic roots of the people of the British Isles and Japan. He discovered DNA could be categorised into seven basic groups, and these, he hypothesised came from just seven women. He calls these women the "Seven Daughters of Eve." He has named these 'clan mothers' Helena, Tara, Jasmine, Xenia, Velda, Katherine, and Ursula. Sykes found that 95% of Europeans could be traced back to these ancient 'clan mothers', and through mutations, determined that these women lived somewhere from 45,000 to 17,000 years ago.

Through tracking the DNA of these 'clan mothers', it was verified that the ancestors of the Irish came from the Iberian Peninsula. There was also a direct correlation of similar DNA among men in Ireland and surveys of Y-chromosomes among the Basque people (north-eastern Spain) and the people of Galicia (north-western Spain and northern Portugal). The male Y-chromosome evidence found by Dr. Sykes also determined that the Irish Gaelic tribes first journeyed to the Argyll area of Scotland. There seems to have been a gradual colonisation of the western part of Scotland from the Irish kingdom of

Dál Riada, during the first half of the first millennium CE, which had a huge cultural impact on Scotland, changing its history and bequeathing it the Scottish language, a variant of the Irish language. This would seem to correlate well with the medieval accounts of John of Fordun and Walter Bower, who claim that the progenitors of the Scottish race came from Spain, via Ireland.

ARRIVAL IN IRELAND

From the previous chapter we know that Meritaten/Scotia is said to have travelled to Ireland from Spain, this is detailed in the accounts of both John of Fordun and Walter Bower. However, both writers were mostly concerned with the history of Scotland, so it is to the Irish accounts that we must turn. We are already familiar with 'Lebor Gabála Erenn' (The Book of the Taking of Ireland) also known as the Book of Invasions. This book has three different versions of many stories and it is very much regarded as a pseudo-history. However, one can only assume that portions of it at least, are based on real events, long forgotten and retold with little regard for accuracy. Fortunately, it is not the only Irish source of 'information' about Scotia/Scota and what happened to her and her entourage in Ireland. 'The Book of Leinster', compiled around 1160 CE, contains a version of the story, supposedly a redaction of the version in 'Lebor Gabála Erenn'. We also find mention of Scotia in the work of Seathrún Céitinn, or in English, Geoffrey Keating (circa 1569 – 1644 CE). Keating is said to have attended a bardic school at Burgess, County Tipperary, which was attributed to the Bard Tomás Ó Súilleabháin. Following the collapse of Irish resistance after the Nine Years War with England, Keating left Ireland, in November 1603, one of forty students who sailed to the Irish College in Bordeaux, under the supervision of the Rev. Diarmaid MacCarthy.

Keating returned to Ireland after his studies and finished work on 'A Complete History of Ireland' (Foras Feasa ar Éirinn) around 1634 CE. Although greatly dismissed by Protestant scholars of the time, due to his pro-Catholic tendencies, Keating was a highly educated man and produced five major works during his life. Modern re-evaluation of his erudition would be less dismissive now that former religious prejudice has dramatically declined.

This is a rather long extract from his work 'A Complete History of Ireland', but it strongly argues the point of the name Scotia being common to both Scotland and Ireland, going back to before the Dál Riada Scottish kingdom was established.

"Section 48 (XLVIII)

Niall Naoighiallach son of Eochaidh Muighmheadhon, son of Muireadhach Tireach, son of Fiachaidh Sraibhthine, son of Cairbre Lithfeachair, son of Cormac Ulfhada, son of Art Aoinfhear, son of Conn Ceadchathach of the race of Eireamhon, held the sovereignty of Ireland twenty-seven years. Cairionn Chasdubh, daughter of the king of Britain, was Niall's mother. Inne daughter of Lughaidh, wife of Niall, was the mother of Fiachaidh. A second wife of Niall's was Rioghnach, who bore him seven sons, namely, Laoghaire and Eanna, Maine, Eoghan, two Conalls, and Cairbre, as the poet says in this stanza:—

Joyous was the bright Rioghnach
When she bore Laoghaire son of Niall,
Eanna, Maine of bright deeds,
Eoghan, two Conalls, Cairbre.

This Niall went into Alba with a large host to strengthen and to establish the Dal Riada and the Scotic race in Alba, who were at this time gaining supremacy over the Cruithnigh, who are called Picti; and he was the first to give the name Scotia to Alba, being requested to do so by the Dal Riada and the Scotic race, on the condition that she should be called Scotia Minor or Lesser Scotia, while Ireland should be termed Scotia Major or Greater Scotia; and it was through veneration for Scota daughter of Pharao Nectonibus, who was wife of Galamh called Milidh of Spain, from whom they themselves sprang, that the Dal Riada chose the name of Scotia for Alba, instead of calling her Hibernia.

Camden states in his chronicle of Britain that Lesser Scotia was the name of Alba, and Greater Scotia the name of Ireland, and says that it cannot be proved by documents that the Albanians were called Scots till the time of the emperor Constantine the Great. Moreover, Camden gives the Irish the name of Scotorum Attavi, that is, the Forbears of the Scots, thus declaring that the Scots of Alba sprang from the Irish. Thus too he speaks on the same subject: The Scots,(says he,) came from Spain to Ireland in the fourth age. {Scoti ex Hispania in Hiberniam quarta aetate venerunt.}''

Besides, Nennius, a British author says, according to Camden, that: *"it was in the fourth age of the world that the Scithae - that is, the Scotic race - took possession of Ireland. Moreover, it is plain from the annals of Ireland that Alba was the name of that country up to the time of Niall Naoighiallach; and when the Dal Riada were permitted to call it Scotia, themselves and their descendants kept on that name. Before that time Alba or Albania was the country's name, from Albanactus, third son of Brutus, since it was Alba that fell to him as his share from his father. Now Brutus had three sons according to Monomotensis, namely Laegrus, Camber, and Albanactus; and Brutus divided the island of Great Britain between them; and to Laegrus he gave Laegria, which derives its name from him, and it is this country which is now called Anglia; to Camber he gave Cambria, which is now called Wales; and the third portion to Albanactus, from whom Alba is called Albania.*

Niall marched after this with his full host from Alba to Laegria, and made an encampment there; and he sent a fleet to Brittany in France, which is called Armorica, for the purpose of plundering that country; and they brought two hundred noble youths as captives to Ireland with them; and it was in this captivity that they brought Patrick, who was sixteen years old, with them, and his two sisters Lupida and Darerca and many other captives besides.

Many authors testify that Scota was the name of Ireland, and that it was the Irish who were called the Scotic race. Thus does Jonas the abbot, in the second chapter, treating of Columcille, speak: Colman, (he says,) who is called Colum, was born in Hibernia, which is inhabited by the Scotic race. {Columbanus qui et Columba vocatur in Hibernia ortus est; eam Scotorum gens incoluit.}'

Beda also, in the first chapter of the first book of the History of Sacsa, says that Ireland was the native land of the Scots. He speaks thus: Hibernia is the true fatherland of the Scots. {Hibernia propria Scotorum patria est.}'"

The same author, writing about the saints, makes a remark which agrees with this. He speaks thus:

It was from Hibernia, the island of the Scots, that St. Kilian and his two companions came. {Sanctus Kilianus et duo socii eius ab Hibernia Scotorum insula venerunt.}

From this it is to be inferred that the Irish were called the Scotic race in the time of Beda, who lived 700 years after Christ. Orosius also, who lived within 400 years after Christ, agrees with the same statement. He thus speaks in the second chapter of the first book: It is the Scotic races that inhabit Ireland. {Hibernia a Scotorum gentibus colitur.}'

And it is plain that the country which is called Ireland used to be called by authors Scotia. Serarius, writing of St. Kilian, speaks thus: Holy Kilian of the Scotic race, etc.''; and immediately after he uses these words, Scotia, which is also called 'Hibernia'. {Beatus Kilianus Scotorum genere et relqa.}'

From this it may be inferred that Scotia was a name for Ireland in constant use like Hibernia. The truth of this matter will be seen from the words of Capgrave, writing of St. Colum; he speaks thus: Scotia was an ancient name of Ireland, whence came the Scotic race, who inhabit that part of Alba which lies nearest to greater Britain; and that Alba is now for this reason called Scotia from Ireland, from which they derive their origin, and whence they immediately came. {Hibernia enim antiquitus Scotia dicta est, de qua gens Scotorum Albaniam Britanniae maiori proximam quae ab eventu modo Scotia dicitur inhabitans, originem duxit et progressum habuit.}

Marianus Scotus, a Scotic author, writing of St.Kilian, agrees with this. He speaks thus: Although that part of Britain which adjoins Sacsa on the north is now properly called Scotia, nevertheless Beda shows that Ireland was formerly known by that name; for when he states that the Pictish race came from Scythia to Ireland, he adds that it was the Scotic race they found there before them. {Etiamsi hodie Scotia proprie vocetur ea Britanniae pars quae ipsi Angliae contigens ad Septentrionem vergit, olim tamen eo nomine Hiberniam notatam fuisse ostendit D. Beda, cum Scythia Pictorum gentem in Hiberniam venisse ait ibique Scotorum gentem invenisse.}

And since it was from the Scotic race the country was named, Scotia was its name at that time. It is to be inferred also from the words of Caesarius, who lived within 500 years after Christ, that Scotia was the name of Ireland. He thus speaks in the twelfth book of the *Dialogues, chap 38: Whoever doubts the existence of Purgatory, let him go to Scotia, and go into the Purgatory of St. Patrick, and he will no longer doubt of the pains of Purgatory. {Qui de Purgatorio dubitat, Scotiam pergat, Purgatorium Sancti Patricii intret, et de Purgatorii poenis amplius non dubitabit.}*

From the words of this author it is to be inferred that Scotia was a common name for Ireland at that time, as there is no place in Alba called Patrick's Purgatory; and it is plain that the place so called is in Ireland; and hence that it was Ireland Caesarius called Scotia. Serarius, writing on St. Bonifacius, is in accord with this: Scotia was also a name for Ireland. However, since there came from the same land of Ireland a certain race to the east of Britain, where the Picti were dwelling, and there they settled down along with them, and at first were called Dalrheudini (that is, Dal Riada), from their own leader Rheuda (that is, Cairbre Rioghfhada), as Beda affirms. But after this they routed the Picti themselves; and they occupied the entire northern portion of that country; and they gave it the old name of their race, so that there is but one Scotic race. There are, however, two Scotias: one of them, the elder and proper Scotia, is Ireland, and the other, which is recent, is the northern part of Britain. *{Hibernia Scotiae sibi nomen etiam vindicabat, quia tamen ex Hibernia ista Scotorum pars quaedam egressa est in eaque Britanniae ora quam Picti iam habebant consederunt; ii quidem principio a duce suo Rheuda Dalrheudini dicti fuerunt, ut ait V. Beda; postea tamen Pictos inde ipsos exegerunt, et boreale totum illud latus obtinuerunt, eique vetus gentus suae nomen indiderunt. Ita ut Scotorum gens una fuerit, sed Scotia duplex facta sit, una vetus et propria in Hibernia, recentior altera in septentrionali Britannia.}*

I note three things from the words of the author. The first of these is that the Irish are truly the Scots; the second is that it was the Dal Riada that were first called Scots in Alba, since it was they who first conquered the Picti in Alba. The third is that he says that Ireland was the older Scotia, and Alba the new Scotia, and that it was the Scotic race who first called it Scotia. Buchanan, a Scotch author, in the second book of the History of Scotland, makes a statement which bears out the author quoted above. He speaks thus: The inhabitants of Ireland were called Scots, as Orosius points out, and as our own annals record; it was not once only the Scots migrated from Ireland to Alba. {Scoti omnes Hiberniae habitatores initio vocabantur ut indicat Orosius, nec semel Scotorum ex Hibernia transitum in Albiam factum nostri annales referunt.}'

From this it is to be inferred that it was not the Dal Riada alone who went from Ireland to settle in Alba, but numerous other tribes as well from time to time."

Keating's work is, of course, based on the surviving Irish texts of the time, like Fordun and Bower before him, he was far removed from the events he was writing about. The early Irish sources were compiled much earlier than the Scottish ones, some as early as the 6th century CE, some 1000 years before Keating wrote the most famous of his books.

We shall return to the familiar 'Lebor Gabála Erenn', but before doing so, I will refer to another of the ancient Irish annals, which mentions the 'Scots' on many occasions. It also describes the arrival of Scotia and her entourage in Ireland, in a section on declensions of the Irish language. This book, entitled 'Auraicept na nÉces' (or 'The Scholar's Primer' in English), is primarily about the Irish language and the Ogham alphabet (used to write Gaeilge/Irish) and the bulk of this text is Old Irish from the early 8th century CE, but which had considerable additions over the next five hundred years. For a book on language, it is perhaps surprising to find mention of Scota, however this book goes much further back, in its aim to trace the origins as far as the biblical Tower of Babel.

"Of the origins of the declensions here below.

The beginning of letters, verse-feet, declensions, accents, intervals, genders, and comparisons as they were established by poets of the same school in which they dwelt, and by Fenius Farsaidh after the selection of Gaelic out of the 72 languages. Hence it was attributed to Goedel son of Angen, for it was he that desired the selection of Gaelic, to wit, the one language that was more beautiful and excellent than any language, so that for this reason it used to serve, and therefore it was attributed, so that hence Gaelic and the Gael are named. Nel, or Nin, son of Fenius it was who married Scota, daughter of Pharaoh, so that it is from her name they are called Scots."

Another work of note is that of Roderick O'Flaherty (Ruaidhrí Ó Flaithbheartaigh), whose major work 'Ogygia: seu, rerum Hibernicarum chronologia' was published in Latin in 1685 CE. He was the last Irish Lord of Connacht and final chief of the O'Flaherty clan. Most of his hereditary lands had been confiscated from his Father, before his birth, during the Cromwellian land confiscations. Being a Catholic, a Stuart supporter and a member of the Irish Gaelic nobility, it was no great surprise that O'Flaherty's Ogygia was heavily criticised by the Protestant Ascendancy and the English establishment. Its publication was during a time of turmoil and civil war in both Ireland and Britain. The deposing of the Stuart line of Scottish kings and their replacement with a Dutch (but Protestant) interloper took place a mere 3 years after the book was published. After a lengthy pre-amble to the main text of the book itself, O'Flaherty mentions the Scots almost immediately:

"THE PREFACE TO THE READER

I have been the more induced to entitle this rich chronology Scottish one, as it particularly treats of the nation of the Scots, who, in the reign of Solomon, at Jerusalem, emigrating hither, have enjoyed an unalienated sovereignty above two thousand years, governed by their own laws until the English constitution was established here, under the auspices of king James; and they fill boast of kings of Scottish origin, from the line of that James. Hence, with the old Latin writers, Scotia, and the island of the Scots, has been derived from the people residing there : but a colony of the Scots going over to North Britain, after some time acquired a very extensive and potent kingdom, which for some centuries has been solely and only known by the name of Scotia: so that it is disputed by some, but very improperly, whether Ireland was ever called Scotia. In consequence of which, modern Scots writers have taken occasion to attribute to their own countrymen whatever they have read in history relative to the Scots, and to form a very long series of kings from the reign of Alexander the Great.

...which, concerning the very ancient royal line of this princes, and the antiquity of her nation, is not only worthy of poetical credit, but founded on the firm basis of historical veracity; except that the modern daughter assumes and adopts the age of the parent

Scotia, and both participate of that antiquity, by the daughter's succeeding the mother. This poet, in the above mentioned Epithalamium, following the torrent of contemporary historians, under the pretext of the modern acceptation of the Scottish name, ascribes to his countrymen the colleges and abbeys the Irish, the the appellation of Scots..."

So clearly, O'Flaherty links the Irish and the Scots as more-or-less the same race of people since antiquity. Given the known history of the two countries, it would appear that he is definitely correct, at least as far back as the early 5th century CE, with the establishment of the Gaelic kingdom of Dál Riada. Earlier links are much harder to prove historically, but given the very short distance between eastern Ulster and western Scotland, travel between the two places may have been commonplace much earlier than is officially acknowledged.

O'Flaherty goes on to mention Roman accounts, linking the modern Gaels of Scotland and Ireland with an ancient progenitor coming to both places, from Spain.

"Caesar, (well informed by the opportunities he had of making himself acquainted with the manners and customs of the Gauls) writes, that in Gaul the people were divided into three scepts or tribes, and that each spoke a language peculiar to itself, so that it is absurd to think, that a Scot, who was an adventurer from Spain, should find his mother-tongue to agree, and be similar to the language used by the inhabitants of this clime, as it is universally recorded, that they were of a different family from Fenius, from whom the Scots deduce their existence and language. But, after recurring to those dark and unenlightened ages, and to

the condensed clouds of ignorance and fable which had guided the writers of those times, we can give the following account, omitting a variety and multiplicity of long and tedious voyages. and expeditions from Scythia, Greece, and Thrace."

Further on he expresses his views on Egyptian connections:

"Now I am of opinion, that we should give some degree of credit and belief to the investigations of our antiquarians, which prove that Aeria and Ogygia were given in common to Egypt and Ireland, and to that other most ancient and universally allowed tradition of our historians, of the marriage of Scota, the daughter of Pharaoh, with a predecessor of the Scots : which evidently convinces us that there had been a commerce and an alliance of a very ancient date carried on, and mutually maintained, between the Egyptians and our ancestors; and which, if they have not subsisted when Pharaoh was immersed in the Red Sea, or when Moses with some one or other of the succeeding Pharaohs."

O'Flaherty mentions Míl who he here refers to as Milesius on a few occasions, but there is only one extract of note:

"The Scots, who are likewise denominated Gaidelians, a Scythian colony from Cantabria, a province of citerior Spain, arriving in Ireland by the bay of Biscay next to Ireland, and by Lepisca contiguous to Navarre, and the Pyrenean mountains. I say, landing in the southern parts of the kingdom, where Kerry in the fouth of Munster lies adjacent to the ocean, at length totally subdued the Dananns in the battle of Talten. From that time, they ruled this island by long, successive, and extensive posterity. Five colonies preceded them; as the Partholans, and

the Nemethians, the empire of the Belgians and Dananns, and the incursions of the Fomorians. The kings of the Scottish line were defended from the three sons of the Spanish soldier, or Milesius : to wit, Heber, Hir and Herimon; except three from Ith, the uncle of Milesius, and one from the people. The Antiquarians have remarked, that a hundred years have clapsed from this epoch of the Scottish era to the end of the reign of Tigernmas, king of Ireland and 230 to the triumph Aeneas Olmacad, king of Ireland over the Picts."

Of course, there is the view that O'Flaherty, Keating, Fordun and Bower, amongst others were using false or 'pseudo-histories' as their primary sources, and hence all their arguments are illogical and unproven. While it is true that they used the doubtful Irish and Scottish sources, they also made use of whatever sources of the 'Old World' in Latin and Greek that were available at the time. These writers may be regarded with scepticism today, but in their own eras they were very well educated and serious scholars. Much of the negative opinions about their work originated from imperial and religious prejudice of the British establishment. It is only in the light of translations of works written in Egyptian hieroglyphics and cuneiform (from the modern era), modern archaeology and DNA analysis that we can form a more accurate opinion of the veracity of their accounts and the works they used as source material.

This brings me to my final excerpt, which is from the 'Lebor Gabála Erenn' (The Book of the Taking of Ireland), mentioned many times previously and which is probably the oldest of the Irish or Scottish sources that still exists.

"Now, this is what learned men relate; that thirty-six leaders and nobles strong the Gáedil came. [Each of them had a ship, which makes thirty(-six) ships.] And four-and-twenty servitors had they, each of whom had a ship; and four-and-twenty servitors along with every servitor in every ship, again. These are the six and thirty chieftains who came into Ireland.

As Fintan s. Bochra recorded (who was born seven years before the Flood; till seven years of the reign of Diarmait mac Cerbaill, that was his [Fintan's] life). Under the nurture of Finnian of Mag Bile, and of Colum Cille, and a Túan mac Cairill recorded in the presence of the Irish and of Finnian of Mag Bile, And as their pupils related, to wit Ladeend s. Bairche, and Colmán s. Comgellán, and Cenn Fáelad s. Ailill, and Senchan s. Colmán, Cú Alad from the Cruachans, and Bran of Boirenn, etc. Those are the pupils of Finnian and of Túan.

And what they said was, that these are the thirty-six chieftains who entered Ireland as the Gáedil, namely the ten sons of Bregon (Íth being one of them) – Brego, Bile, Blad, Cualu, Cuailnge, Fúat, Muirthemne, Eibleo, Íth, Nár: the single son of Bile, Míl of Spain (Galam was his proper name): the seven sons of Míl, Donn, Colptha, Amorgen, Éber, Ír, Érimón, Érech Febria and Érennán, the youngest of the family. The three sons of Érimón; Muimne, Luigne, Laigne; and also Palap and Írial Fáid (but in Ireland itself was Írial born), the son of Érimón.

And he is called Nuadu Airgetlám. Nuadu Airgetlám had two sons, Glas a quo Síl nArgetrois, and Fir Nuadat; and they took the princedom over Ireland; for Nuadu was not in partnership with them, for he was a youth, and there was no disturbance of division among them, on account of his piety to his brethren; but he used to feed and…

They had forty chieftains; Eber Donn s. Míl, and Eremón, who were two in joint rule over Spain at the time. Here are the names of the kings and chieftains who came: Brego s. Breogan, the eldest eponymus of Mag Breg; Cualu s. Breogan eponymus of Sliab Cualann; Cuailnge s. Breogan, eponymus of Sliab Cuailnge; Blad s. Breogan, eponymus of Sliab Bladma; Fúat s. Breogan, eponymus of Sliab Fúait; Muirthemne s. Breogan, eponymus of Mag Muirthemne; Lugaid s. Íth, who came to avenge his father, from whom comes Corco Laigde; Eiblinne s. Breogan, eponymus of Sliab Eiblinne; Búas, Bres, Buaigne, the three sons of Tigernbard s. Brig s. Breogan; Nár eponymus of Ros Náir in Sliab Bladma; Ér, Orba, Ferón, Fergna, the four sons of Brig s. Breogan; Fulmán, Mantán, Caicher s. Mantán, Suirge s. Caicher; Én, Ún and Etán; Lui s. Brig s. Brego s. Breogan; Sobairche, we know not his father; Bile s. Brigi s. Breogan; Míl of Spain with his eight sons – Érimón, Éber, Ír, Donn the king, Amorgen the poet, Colptha, Airech Febria, and Érannán the youngest. The five sons of Érimón, Muimne, Luigne, Laigne, Palap, Írial Fáid (but in Ireland was Írial born)."

The rather cumbersome list of descendants and ancestors that fills much of the text was common of literature of this time, the genealogy of those involved being considered of vital importance. Most of these characters are irrelevant as regards the life of Scotia, but we can note the mention of the deceased Bile, and his father Breogan and the presence (in Ireland) of Bile's son Míl (Míl Espáine/Milesius), Íth (son of Breogan) who dies in Ireland and Amorgen (Amergin Glúingel) who is the legendary poet of the Gaels and one of Míl's sons.

The stories given in 'Lebor Gabála Erenn' are long and complex, not an easy read by any means, but the bare bones of the events I will describe concisely. The Milesians landed at the estuary of Inber Scéne, so named after Amergin's deceased wife Scéne. Amergin appears to be the main protagonistm after some failures, and secures the permission of the three tutelary Goddesses of Ireland (Banba, Ériu and Fódla) for him and his people to settle in Ireland. Each of the three goddesses required Amergin to name the island after each of them, which he did. The goddess Ériu is the origin of the modern Irish name Éire. 'Éirinn' is the dative case of the Irish word for Ireland, the genitive is 'Éireann' and the modern female name Erin is also derived from the name of the goddesses Ériu. Banba and Fódla are largely forgotten today but they have been used as poetic names for Ireland, in much the same way as Alba was used for Scotland and Albion was for the island Britain.

The Milesians had to win the island by engaging in battle with the three kings of the Tuatha Dé Danann, their druids and army of warriors. It was Amergin who acted as an impartial judge for the waring parties, setting the rules of engagement. The Milesians agreed to leave the island and retreat a short distance back into the ocean, beyond the ninth wave, regarded as magical boundary. However, having secured the permission of the goddesses, they made to return to the beach, but the druids of the Tuatha Dé Danann invoked a magical storm to prevent them from returning. Amergin sang the now famous invocation 'The Song of Amergin', calling upon the spirit of Ireland and thus was able to quell the storm and bring the ship safely to land on the Dingle Peninsula, in western county Kerry. The war continued from there and there were heavy losses on both sides. Eventually the Milesians defeated the Tuatha Dé Danann and conquered the whole island. The three kings of the Tuatha Dé Danann were each killed (in single combat), one by one, by three of the surviving sons of Míl, including Amergin himself.

There are several translations of The Song of Amergin, by Lady Gregory (Isabella Augusta Persse), R.A.S. MacAllister and Robert Graves, but the most recent, and probably most reliable, is that of James Carey, taken from the 'Book of Leinster' (Lebar na Núachongbála). Below is his translation, taken from his book 'The Celtic Heroic Age', which was co-written with John T. Kotch.

"I am a wind in the sea (for depth)
I am a sea-wave upon the land (for heaviness)
I am the sound of the sea (for fearsomeness)
I am a stag of seven combats (for strength)
I am a hawk upon a cliff (for agility)
I am a tear-drop of the sun (for purity)
I am fair (i.e. there is no plant fairer than I)
I am a boar for valour (for harshness)
I am a salmon in a pool (for swiftness)
I am a lake in a plain (for size)
I am the excellence of arts (for beauty)
I am a spear that wages battle with plunder.
I am a god who froms subjects for a ruler
Who explains the stones of the mountains?
Who invokes the ages of the moon?
Where lies the setting fo the sun?
Who bears cattle from the house of Tethra?

Who are the cattle of Tethra who laugh?
What man, what god forms weapons?
Indeed, then;
I invoked a satirist...
a satirist of wind."

Here below is the excerpt from 'Lebor Gabála Erenn', which eventually brings us to Scotia/Scota and her death. However, this event forms a very minor part of the story and is not given the great fanfare that one might expect.

"And his grave is in Inber Scéne, and the grave of Scéne wife of Amorgen on the other side. She died on the sea at their estuary, and Amorgen said: The harbour wherein we shall land, shall bear the name of Scéne. The sons of Míl made a contention in rowing as they came to Ireland from the place where they saw Ireland away from them; and Ír son of Míl advanced the length of a murchrech beyond every ship. Éber Donn, the eldest of the family, was envious, and he said –

It is not lucky that Ír leapeth beyond Íth,

– [that is, beyond Lugaid son of Íth]. Then the oar that was in the hand of Ír broke, so that he fell backward, and died in the following night; and his body was taken to Sceilie, behind the Southern promontory of Corco Duibne.

Every time that the Sons of Míl came up with Ireland, the demons would frame that the port was, as it were, a hog's back; whence Ireland is called "Hog Island". They skirted around Ireland three times, and landed at last in Inber Scéne.

Sorrowful were Éber Finn and Érimón and Amorgen after the death of their brother; and they said: It were right that Éber Donn should have no share of the land regarding which he was envious of his brother Ír. On the morrow Scéne and Érannán were buried in Inber Scéne. They two were both buried; their mounds and their graves are still there, side by side...

At the end of three days and three nights thereafter, the sons of Míl broke the battle of Sliab Mis against demons and Fomoraig, that is, against the Túatha Dé Danann. It is there that Fás (sic lege) fell, the wife of Ún s. Uicce, after whom "the grave of Fás" is named, between Sliab Mis and the sea.

Scota d. Pharao, King of Egypt, also died in that battle – the wife of Érimón s. Míl. For Míl s. Bile went a-voyaging into Egypt, four ships' companies strong, and he took Scota to wife, and Érimón took her after him. In that night on which the sons of Míl came into Ireland, was the burst of Loch Luigdech in Iar-Mumu.

"Sliab Mis" – that means the worst mountain which they found after coming into Ireland, for there they fought their first battle in Ireland."

She is mentioned again, further in the text, in one of the other versions of the story contained in the book.

"And they left namely the flower of their queens likewise on the same occasion. Fás wife of Ún s. Ucce fell - from her named 'The Grave of Fás' and 'Glenn Fáise' between Sliabh Mis and the sea. Scotia daughter of the Pharaoh of Egypt, wife of Érimón, died also in that battle; Míl was her father - sic in aliis libris inuenitur (so it is found in other books)."

On the pages that follow, is another version:

"When the sons of Mil reached their landing-place they made no delay until they reached Sliab Mis; and the battle of Sliab Mis was fought between them and the Tuatha De Danann, and the

victory was with the sons of Mil. Many of the Tuatha De Dannan were killed in that battle. It is there that Fas wife of Un son of Uicce fell, from whom is named Glen Faise. Scota wife of Mil fell in the same valley; from her is named " Scota's Grave", between Sliab Mis and the sea. The sons of Mil went afterwards to Tailltiu, and another battle was fought between them and the Tuatha De Danann there."

Further on again in the text, we find an interesting poem that describes the exploits of the Milesians and we find mentions of Scota again:

"Of the adventures of the Gaedels from the time when they went from Scythia till they took Ireland and the division of Ireland between them, with their chieftains, the poet Roigne Roscadach son of Ugaine Mor said to Mal son of Ugaine his brother, when Mal questioned him: "Sing thy description in the great knowledge of Ireland, O Roigne," Roigne answered him and said:

O noble son of Ugaine,
How does one arrive at knowledge of Ireland,
The conquest of its company?
Before they overflowed Scythia
They reached the host-king of Shinar;

They approached Egypt,
Where Cingeris was extinguished,
So that a great troop was destroyed,
Who died in the Red Sea.

They flowed through a space very faithful,
With Pharaoh fought;
Niul contracts with Scota,
The conception of our fathers.

They took the name "Gaedels,"
The name "Scots" spreads,
The fair daughter of Pharaoh.

They overspread lands,
Burst into Scythia,
Determined long combat-
The Children of Nel and Noenbal.

Golam was a young lord,
Who slew the son of Neman,
Escaped to Egypt,
Where was Nectanebus.

Pharaoh was welcoming
To Golam; gave
A marriage Nectanebus,
Scota was at cot's head;

A name was changed from them.
They advanced past Africa,
Good was the man under whom they trembled;
Fenius Farsad, the keen,
Well he spread for us a lasting name.

They approached Spain,
Where was born a numerous progeny,
Donn, Airech, Amergin,
Eber, Ir, Colptha himself,

Eremon, Erannan,
The eight sons of Golam.
Mil's renown came upon them,
The sons of Mil wealthy;

Their scholars resolved,
Divided ships,
The Men returned from the burial of Fial.
They divided Ireland,
In twice six, an inheritance of chieftains.

Seek the truth of every law,
Relate sharply the inquiry, O Son!

The two sons of Mil, famous in dignity,
Took Ireland and Britain;
With them there followed hither
A gentle poet and a harper.

Cior son of Cis, the bright poet,
The name of the harper Cennfin;
With the sons of Mil, of bright fame,
The harper sounded his harp.

The princes, with many battles,
Took the kingdom of Ireland;
They did it with brightness, merry the sound,
Eber and Eremon."

One further account (worthy of mention) of Scotia and the origins of the Milesians comes from "The Settling of The Manor at Tara" (Incipit do Suidigud Tellaich Temra), which was published in English in 1910.

This story came from the time of Irish High King Diarmait mac Cerbaill, who died circa 565 CE. In the story the party are concerned to know the origins of the Gaels (Milesians) who are their ancestors. All manner of people are called, but finally Fintan is called, who has the story, an ancient man of great wisdom as well as age:

"Then Berran, Cennfaelad's attendant, went for Fintan to Dun Tulcha to the west of Luachair Dedaid. And he delivered his message to him. Then Fintan came with him to Tara. And his retinue consisted of eighteen companies, namely, nine before him and nine behind. And there was not one among them who was not of the seed of Fintan—sons, grandsons, great-grandsons, and descendants of his was that host...

...After that came the sons of Míl
out of Spain from the south,
and I lived along with them
though mighty was their combat.

I had attained to long life,
I will not hide it,

when the Faith came to me
from the King of the cloudy heaven.

I am white Fintan,
Bóchra's son, I will not hide it.
Since the Deluge here
I am a high noble sage."

Fintan, including some lengthy biblical references and geneological listings and a history of Ireland from its earliest days, goes on to explain that he was alive at that time and in the party that arrived on Ireland's shores.

"'Say then,' said he, 'what is your race, and whence have ye come into this island?' 'Easy to say,' said Conaing Bececlach. 'From the children of Míl of Spain and from the Greeks are we sprung. After the building of the Tower of Nimrod, and the confusion of tongues, we came into Egypt, upon the invitation of Pharaoh King of Egypt. Nél son of Fénius and Goedel Glas were our chiefs while we were in the south. Hence we are called Féne from Fénius, that is the Féne, and Gaels from Gaedel Glas, as was said:'

The Féne from Fénius are named, meaning without straining,
the Gaels from Gaedel Glas the hospitable, the Scots from Scota.
'Scota, then, the daughter of Pharaoh the king was given as a
wife to Nél son of Fénius on going into Egypt. So that she is our
ancestress, and it is from her we are called Scots.'

...'In the night then in which the children of Israel escaped out of Egypt, when they went with dry feet through the Red Sea with the leader of the people of God, even Moses son of Amram, and when Pharaoh and his host were drowned in that sea, having kept the Hebrews in

bondage, because our forefathers went not with the Egyptians in pursuit of the people of God, they dreaded Pharaoh's wrath against them should he return, and even if Pharaoh should not return they feared that the Egyptians would enslave them as they had enslaved the children of Israel on another occasion. So they escaped in the night in ten of Pharaoh's ships upon the strait of the Red Sea, upon the boundless ocean, and round the world north-west, past the Caucasus mountains, past Scythia and India, across the sea that is there, namely the Caspian, over the Palus Maeotis, past Europe, from the south-east to the south-west along the Mediterranean, left-hand to Africa, past the Columns of Hercules to Spain, and thence to this island.'

And Spain,' said Trefuilngid, 'where is that land?'

'Not hard to say. It is the distance of a great prospect from us to the south,' said Conaing. 'For it is by a view (?) Ith son of Breogan saw the mountains of southern Irrus from the top of the tower of Breogan in Spain, and he it is who came to spy out this island for the sons of Míl, and on his track we came into it, in the ninth year after the passage of the Israelites through the Red Sea.'

'How many are you in this island?' said Trefuilngid.

'I should like to see you assembled in one place.' 'We are not so few indeed,' replied Conaing, 'and if thou desirest it, so shall it be done; only I think it will distress the people to support thee during that period.' 'It will be no distress,' said he, 'for the fragrance of this branch which is in my hand will serve me for food and drink as long as I live.'

As others have done, this account refers to the Pharaoh of the time of Moses, Ramesses II, but this is a common mistake, and an afirming one, as it links the story with The Old Testament, which writers of the time commonly did. The story is in both the 'Yellow Book of Lecan' and in the 'Book of Lismore', the earliest version of which is late 14th century CE. In the text, there is a clear belief that the Gaels are descendants of Scota, arriving in Ireland from Egypt, via Spain.

What is apparent is that there are not just one or two accounts of Scotia/Scota, or the belief that she came with the Gaels (Milesians) to Ireland - there are several accounts, across different time periods, each with their own variations.

So, in conclusion, from both the ancient texts, dating to the 6th century CE and those of later writers, in the late medieval and renaissance period, we can see that there are multiple accounts of Scotia/Scota arriving in Ireland, with a tribe of people from Spain, whose origins are sometimes described as Scythia or Armenia. It is clear from the texts that she was the daughter of a Pharaoh, and she is sometimes described as a queen or as a princess.

In all of the Irish accounts she is given as dying close to Sliabh Mis, at the eastern end of this mountain range that runs along the Dingle Peninsula (which is located in the western part of county Kerry). So here we find what is believed, by many, to be the final resting place of Scotia/Scota, the Egyptian princess/queen who fled Egypt.

From my own research, and that of others, the mysterious Scotia appears to be none other than Meritaten, eldest daughter of the heretical Pharaoh, Akhenaten. Circumstantial evidence and events of the time period lend some support to this theory, but due to the lack of direct evidence, none of this can be proven as yet, no matter how convincing the arguments may be. What is needed to prove the Meritaten-Scotia theory correct is physical evidence of her existence, such as one might find if we had located her remains, in her final resting place.

SCOTIA'S GRAVE

I first heard of Scotia's grave from French illustrator Elena Danaan, around 2015, when she was involved in a project to mark the traditional resting place of Scotia. For unknown reasons, despite the spelling generally being Scota in the oldest Irish texts, in modern Ireland at least, she is generally referred to as Scotia. Even some of the housing estates in the South Tralee area, not too far from the memorial, use the name Scotia, in recognition of her. The creation of a memorial garden and the improvement of a 'heritage trail' around Tralee, including to Scotia's Grave, was completed in 2017. There was considerable publicity in the Tralee area, Tralee being the largest town in Kerry and also the closest to the grave site.

The obelisk was created by local stonemason Billy Leen, who lives only a few kilometres from the garden's location in the townland of Clahane. The obelisk was designed by Elena Danaan who wrote the Egyptian hieroglyphics, carved onto it by Billy Leen. The obelisk is approximately 6 feet tall and it is raised above the level of the road, erected in a small garden area, which is full of shrubs.

This obelisk serves as a marker on the road that leads directly to the farm gate that takes you, on a rather difficult journey, to Scotia's Grave. The area of the grave itself is a few kilometres away from the road, as the crow flies, and is known variously as Foley's Glen, Gleann Scoithín and Feart Scoithín. Local Councillor Pa Daly (now a TD in Dáil Éireann, the Irish Parliament), was a major force in the creation of this project and he is quoted in a local paper as saying the following, at the opening ceremony:

Figure 27: The obelisk in memory of Scotia, created by Billy Leen and Elena Danaan, was officially unveiled in 2017, at the road in Clahane that leads to the walkway to Scotia's Grave.

"I am delighted that the first phase of a motion I moved last year on establishing a heritage trail around Tralee has been implemented, and I would like to compliment both Tidy Tralee Together who were responsible for installing the sculpture, and Billy Leen, the stonemason.

The obelisk points the way towards Scotias grave in Foley's glen, where according to mythology, the Milesians led by Queen Scotia defeated the native Tuatha Dé Danann. I hope that the other heritage attractions around the town, which were known to generations of Tralee people will receive the same recognition in the coming months and years. We owe it to past and future generations to safeguard our heritage and to ensure that places that have endured in the folk memory and are of strong historical importance are recognized and not lost to future generations."

Unfortunately the garden in which the obelisk stands has become badly neglected and, at the time of writing (early 2025), it was so overgrown that part of the obelisk was obscured by plant growth. One can only hope that locals, the Tidy Towns committee, or Kerry County Council will take better care of it in the future.

The entrance to the glen is marked only by a brown sign that points at a simple metal farm gate on the opposite side of the road. The route does not have a clear path, one immediately has to navigate a swampy field to find a rough pathway running south-west towards the grave, crossing a small river several times, over narrow metal foot bridges. In winter-time getting to Leac Scoitín, or Scotia's Grave, can be quite a challenge and even in summer-time wearing wellington boots or sturdy walking boots and rain gear is advisable.

Figure 28: the sign, by the side of the road, pointing to Scotia's Grave (Leac Scoitín) located in Scotia's Glen (Gleann Scoithín).

LEACHT SCOIH I N

Figure 29: the Ogham inscription on the large stone located next to Scotia's Grave, which reads Leacht Scóhin, which equates to 'grave of Scotia'.

On arriving at the site, there is a large outcrop of rock on the right, which has often been mistaken for her gravestone. This rock, rather sadly, is covered in both modern and ancient graffiti, since as obscure as this place is, it has been visited by many people over the last few hundred years at least.

It is supposed that this rock was inscribed with the above message in ogham script. For those, unfamiliar with Ogham, it is an alphabet unique to Ireland, specifically for writing 'as Gaeilge', that is in the Irish language. According to official sources such as the Office of Public Works, Ogham was developed in the 4th century CE, but many people, myself included, believe it was developed possibly much earlier. I believe this mainly due to the many mentions of it in mythology that refers to the Pagan era, in the Bronze Age or early Iron Age.

The Ogham characters are written on a stave running vertically (usually on a tall upright stone) which is read from bottom to top. On paper, or some other medium, Ogham is often written horizontally and it is read from left to right. The words on the rock near the grave, in Irish, when converted to modern Roman script read - Leacht Scóhin, or Leacht Scoihin, similar indeed to the modern name of Leac Scoitín.

At what point in time this incription was carved onto the rock is

Figure 30: the grave of Scotia, which is a small collection of stone that form a rough circle, with a larger central stone.

Figure 31: the grave of Scotia's horse, which is to the left of Scotia's grave, is a less elaborate affair, consisting of a pile of rocks.

unknown, as dating stone is more-or-less impossible, unless it can be tied by the context of the writing itself - to a particular person, event or time period that is known. We know that Scotia/Meritaten would have died in the late 1300s BCE, perhaps anywhere from 1330 - 1300 BCE, as we do not know how long she would have spent in either Spain or Scotland before arriving in Ireland. There is no exact date for the battle of Sliabh Mis, so there is no way of knowing if the Ogham inscription was carved shortly after her death (during that battle), or many centuries later.

American author Ralph Ellis visited Scotia's Grave and was unable to find the Ogham inscription shown in figure 31. On numerous visits, in different weather conditions, I was also unable to locate this inscription, which presumably has been worn away by time and also possibly due to the graffiti on the rock obliterating it. Certainly, there are other inscriptions around Ireland that have faded away to nothing, only known of today because they were recorded or drawn at an earlier date, when they were still visible.

One such example is the famous 'Hag's Chair' at Loughcrew/ Sliabh na Cailleach, which has no visible markings today, but the exact neolithic markings are recorded on paper illustrations, for posterity. If the Ogham inscription was done in the aftermath of the battle of Sliabh Mis then it would be over 3000 years old, which is more than long enough for it to have been eroded by the weather. The grave itself, or rather two graves, are located a short walk from this large stone outcrop, towards the river, in a southerly direction. Local legend is that the two graves are of Scotia and her horse, from which she fell, on the hillside on the opposite side of the small river. The area of the two graves, which are a small stone circle with a central stone (the right-hand one, for

Figure 32: the central stone of Scotia's grave, with an unusual pattern of etched lines carved onto its surface.

Scotia) and a close by pile of large (approximately 20cm) stones, for Scotia's horse.

Both stone monuments are small, the main one being perhaps 2m in diameter and the one to the left (presumably for the horse), around 1m square. On closer inspection, one can see a series of strange lines etched on the central stone of the right-hand (Scotia's) grave. I inspected this stone on more than one occasion, and noticed that when it was very wet a symbol that appeared to be a hieroglyph was visible, which was not apparent during dry weather.

The idea that these stone monuments are graves for Scotia and her horse is purely held in local folklore, there is no exact description of where she died or was buried in any of the ancient literature. They are located in the right place, being at the foothills of the Sliabh Mis mountains, but there is no official recognition of either monument as a grave site. The actual mountain range (Sliabh

Mis) is not the kind of terrain where a pitched battle is likely to have taken place, although Sliabh Mis is home to an ancient, and supposedly impregnable fortress of legendary Munster king Cú Roí mac Dáire, called Caherconree, further west on the Dingle Peninsula. The location of the graves, on the glen, slightly inland from the two coasts north and south of the peninsula and below the mountainous terrain, makes for a plausible battle field. The ancient accounts mention that she was buried 'between Sliabh Mis and the sea', which is so vague that it could be almost anywhere in what is actually a vast area land. In the whole locality there are no similar sites to Leac Scoitín, one has to travel towards Milltown and Castlemaine to find ancient monuments, such as dolmens, but these clearly date from 4000-2000 BCE.

The validity of the site as historically significant is as yet unproven, as no-one has excavated the site to date. In 1999 the National Monuments Service sent a team to take a look at the site and stated: *"Following a site inspection in 1999 it was concluded that the evidence was not sufficient to warrant accepting this as an archaeological monument."*

Personally, I was somewhat mystified by this statement, given that it is clearly the work of human hands in antiquity and has long been regarded as an ancient grave site. However, archaeological work is very expensive, regardless of accessibility. When one considers the site's distance from a road, with no parking facilities, the difficulty of getting to the location, and the difficulty of bringing resources to the site, I am sure that it would prove to be a very costly exercise. With no guarantee of finding anything significant, I imagine that there is little or no desire to go to great expense to excavate the two supposed graves.

It would be wonderful if a team of archaeologists was willing to excavate the site and see if there are any human remains, or any artefacts of interest to be found. While it would be a difficult dig, in terms of logistics, it is a simple enough site, in a small and relatively flat area. Such an effort would throw some light on the local legends of the place and no doubt also give confirmation of the validity, or falsehood, of the stories from the Irish and Scottish annals.

The Central Stone - Inscriptions, Graffiti or Random Lines?
Having visited the site on several occasions, in different conditions, it became apparent that there is a series of indentations in the centre stone of the grave attributed to Scotia. These indentations are clearly the work of humans, but careful analysis is necessary to try to determine if these are random lines, graffiti or something else. I became aware that these indentations were not visible when the stone was dry or merely damp - they only become clearly visible when the stone is very wet, and even then, they are not especially clear. This might be explain why these lines/indentations have never been recorded previously, as they would often-times be invisible or difficult to perceive.

Having traced the outlines, it appears there is a large letter K, although this is possibly modern graffiti, although it might be just a series of 3 lines. To the left there appears to be a horizontal box or lozenge, similar in shape to the Egyptian cartouche. On the right of the 'K' is another box or lozenge, which is smaller and vertically oriented, the corners are very clearly rounded, as is typical of all cartouches. In addition, the white patches on

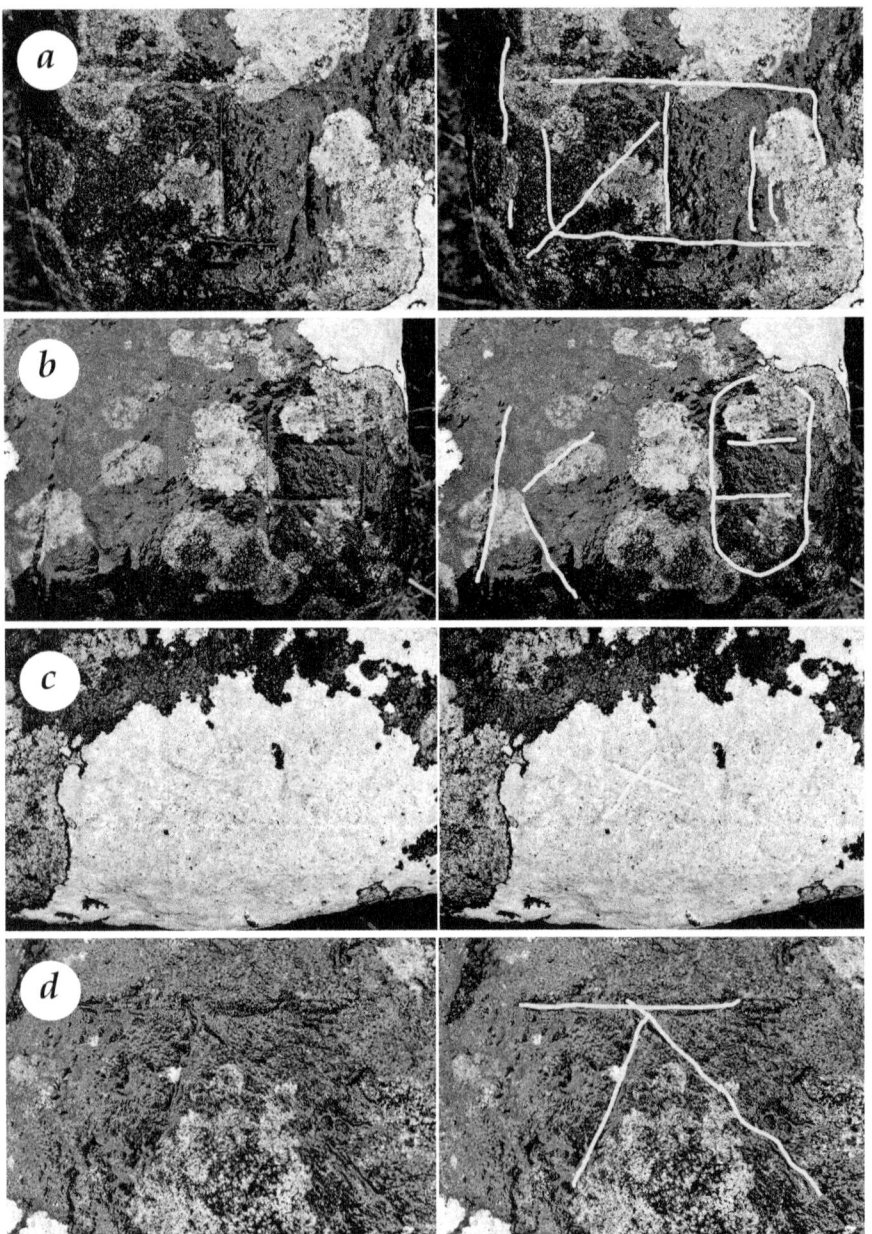

Figure 33 a, b, c and d: carved indentations on the central stone are visible when soaked and are clearly the work of human hands. Interpretation of what these means is difficult, further analysis is required.

the rock appear to be etched or inscribed with lines, but it is not at all easy to make out, although something is clearly there. In addition, a symbol like an upside down 'V' with a line across the point, does closely resemble a known hieroglyphic.

This series of carved lines could of course be a mere coincidence, but how strange it is that the lines on this stone, central to a grave attributed to a daughter on an Egyptian Pharaoh, could have two lozenges etched on it, in the correct shape for a cartouche.

If indeed they are cartouches the hieroglyphs inside them are illegible, and appear to be missing. What is also strange is the straight lines in both lozenges, that are not typically seen within a cartouche. On balance, the poor workmanship inclines me to think that neither box is a cartouche. They could possibly be rudimentary hieroglyphs, or some other symbols, which are as yet unidentified. Without further detailed analysis by professional archaeologists, with the right equipment, it is impossible to say if these are indeed Egyptian cartouches, some other symbols or just some seemingly random lines carved into the stone.

One must wonder, if they are cartouches or, if even one of them is, then what did it once say? If they are something else, then what are they and do these lines and boxes have any significance? It strikes me as unusual to carve lines into a rock for no reason. What is clear is that, with the exception of the 'K', this is not English or Irish graffiti, as it does not represent initials or a name that can be discerned. Someone went to the trouble of carving these indentations into the central stone (and only the central stone), but for what purpose remains unknown at present.

In Egyptian hieroglyphs, a cartouche (called a 'shenu') is an oval with a line at one end of it, this oval is indicative that the text enclosed is a royal name. A cartouche is usually vertical with a horizontal line, but if it makes the name fit better it can be horizontal, with a vertical line at the left end, i.e. in the direction it is read (left to right). The first examples of this are thought to be from pharaohs at the end of the Third Dynasty.

One of the 'boxes' which remsembles the shape of a cartouche is also similar to at least one Egyptian hieroglyph. From comparison of the shapes with hieroglyphs in Faulkner's dictionary of Middle Egyptian, some possiblities presented themselves. However, one has to admit that the level of craftmanship, if the engravings are hieroglyphs, is extremely poor.

The engraving shown in figure 33a is horizontal in the photograph, but I cannot say for sure that this is the correct orientation. If this engraving is flipped 90 degrees then it bears a fair resemblance to a hieroglyph for shrine ('kâr' in Egyptian).

 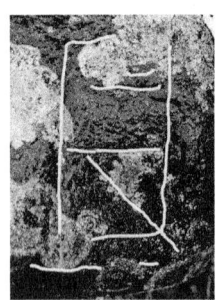

In addition, the engraving in Figure 33d bears a resemblance to the hieroglyphs for 'going' and 'coming' (the word 'ii' in Egyptian), again very roughly carved, but the resemblance is quite striking.

The other symbols that I detected on the stone do not immediately correspond with any hieroglpyths that I looked at (with the kind assistance of Archaeologist Helena Zacharias), but I did not do an exhaustive search of the over one thousand hieroglpyths that existed at the time of the 18th dynasty.

However, even to find two symbols carved on the central stone, that could possibly be Egyptian hieroglyths, is quite amazing. With further analysis of the engravings to see them more clearly, and comparison with a complete list of hieroglyphs, in use from the time period, it may be the case that the engravings are a message, badly written in Middle Egyptian. Without further investigation by experts in this field it is not really possible to give a definitive answer in this regard.

However, given the other indicators, which I have taken pains to discuss in this book, it strikes me as somewhat more than a coincidence that these bizarre etchings (on a stone cube located in a isolated glen in the far west of Ireland) bear any resemblance at all to Middle Egyptian hieroglyphs.

So, I would have to say that the lines on the central stones are fascinating but inconclusive at present, without further investigation. What is clear is that there could be 1 or possibly 2 cartouches etched onto the central stone. This is a possiblity but it is more likely that they are something else. Confirmation would require a team or experts to analyse it carefully to confirm what exactly is present, or may have formerly been visible.

Those familiar with the Egyptian cartouche will know that they were carved to an extremely high standard either in high-relief (cutting in) or bas-relief (embossed), but this is not the case with this central stone, if indeed the markings are a form of cartouche. One can assume that an Egyptian stonemason would have been required among Scotia's entourage, in order to produce an accurate cartouche, in the typical Egyptian style and to the appropriate standard. It may be the case that such a person did not exist and that a poor facsimile or approximation was attempted by the Milesians, who presumably would have been mostly warriors, rather than craftsmen. This cannot be proven in any way, but this theory might explain the roughness and poor artistry, if indeed the markings were an attempt to carve the royal cartouche of Meritaten onto the central stone.

In my discussions (by email) with archaeologist and author Lorraine Evans, she suggested that photogrammetry would be a possible solution to this conundrum. Photogrammetry is defined by the American Society for Photogrammetry and Remote Sensing as "the art, science, and technology of obtaining reliable information about physical objects and the environment, through processes of recording, measuring, and interpreting imagery and digital representations of energy patterns derived from non-contact sensor systems".

This technique goes back to the late 19th century, but has now reached an advanced stage. This is something that I have no expertise in or experience of whatsoever, so it would be necessary for an expert to apply this technique to the central stone at Scotia's grave.

For now, there is no conclusive evidence of Scotia/Meritaten having lived or died in Ireland. The trail I have laid out from Egypt, to Spain, Scotland and Ireland is one that is very probable, in my opinion, but I would prefer to have conclusive proof to offer. Hopefully, at some point in the future, an excavation will take place at Leac Scoitín, including careful analysis of the inscriptions on the central stone. It is this step which will prove the accuracy or inaccuracy of the traditional legends that we are now deeply familiar with. However, at present there are no plans for an academic or archaeological team to visit this site.

Other Evidence of Visitors in Antiquity

So, given that Scotia's Grave remains an unknown quantity, we must look elsewhere for evidence of Egyptians having had an ancient presence in Ireland. There is some evidence, but not a huge amount and, objectively speaking, it doesn't prove much more than that there was some level of trade between Egypt and Ireland, quite possibly through an intermediary, such as the Pheonicians.

In 1955, Dr. Sean O'Riordan an archaeologist at Trinity College, Dublin, was working on excavations of the Mound of Hostages at Tara, site of ancient High Kings (Ard Rí) of Ireland. During this, Bronze Age skeletal remains were found of what has been argued to be a young prince, still wearing a rare necklace of faience beads, made from a paste of minerals and plant extracts that had been fired, which was commonly used in Egypt. In

1956, academics J. F. Stone and L. C. Thomas reported that the faience beads were Egyptian in origin, the beads are currently on display in the National Museum of Ireland, in Dublin:

"In fact, when they were compared with Egyptian faience beads, they were found to be not only of identical manufacture but also of matching design."

Additional analysis by Dr Hugh McKerrel, in 1972 confirms that the faience beads are in fact Egyptian in origin. Dr McKerrel, of the Scottish National Antiquities Museum published his findings in the Proceedings of the Prehistoric Society, which through analysis of the lead content, absolutely proved that the beads came from Egypt from the Eighteen Dynasty period.

The skeleton of the 'Tara Prince' was carbon dated to around 1350 BCE. The necklace found with the remains had a great similarity to a necklace, found around the neck of Pharaoh Tutankhamun (circa 1341 – 1323 BCE). The golden collar around his mummy's neck was also inlayed with matching conical, blue-green faience beads, of similar design.

We already that know Tutankhamun was born roughly around this period of time and that his sister Meritaten had disappeared perhaps 15-20 years after his birth. The discovery of these beads does raise the possibility that there was indeed some immigration in the 14th century BCE from Egypt to the fringes of western Europe, including Ireland. Although in a different country, a very similar necklace was found in a Bronze Age burial mound at north Molton, Devon, the cist grave is thought to be 3800 years old, which would place it at around 1800 - 1700 BCE.

Similar indeed, to the discovery at Tara, was a find made at Knackyboy Cairn at St. Martins in the Isles of Scilly, which is off the south-west coast of Cornwall (southern tip of south-west UK), this is discussed at length by Lorraine Evans in her book 'Kingdom of the Ark'. These excavations took place from 1948 and into the 1950s and yielded five blue faience beads, which are incredibly similar to those found at the Hill of Tara and on the mummy of Pharaoh Tutankhamun.

The original excavation by Bernard St. John O'Neil in 1948 was of a round barrow mound on the uninhabited island. At approximately 15m wide and 1m high it would have been a strange sight to the islanders who did an unofficial excavation themselves in 1912. What St. John O'Neil found was an already disturbed site, with much of the material previously dug over. He explored the stone tunnel inside the mound, which was about 3.5m long and discovered some 22 burial urns, along with a flint axe and the 5 faience beads, in a layer of ancient ashes on the floor of the barrow. Along with this discovery, according to Lorraine Evans, there have been a total of 286 faience beads found in the British Isles (Britain and Ireland), which is by far the most of any European region. This seems to me to be an incredibly large haul of beads and does not lend itself to being some casual occurrence, of no historical or cultural significance. One could assume, perhaps wrongly, that the faience beads from Egypt had arrived in Britain and Ireland purely through trade with Egypt. However, given the burial of these items in a very deliberate manner and the clear evidence from other sources, one must wonder - did these beads belong to actual Egyptians who were present in person in the British Isles at this time period?

Ancient Boat Discoveries in Britain

Another interesting discovery was made, not in Ireland or the Scilly Isles, but in the north-eastern part of Britain. In 1937, North Ferriby, Yorkshire, the remains of an ancient boat were discovered. While it was initially thought to be a Viking longship, continued excavation produced additional ships, wrecked in a storm. Further investigations showed that the boats were much older than the Viking period and were of a type found in the Mediterranean. It was concluded that these boats originated from approximately 3500 years ago and were radiocarbon dated to around 1400 - 1350 BCE. While there is no proof that they were Egyptian vessels, they could well have been of Phoenician or Mycenaean origin. Certainly this find is indicative of international travel by sea, in the time period of the Egyptian Amarna dynasty.

In total, three boats were found, with later datings from 2030 - 1680 BCE, which is much earlier than the Amarna period. The largest of these was over 13m long, big enough for sea voyages. These boats are the oldest known 'sewn-plank boats' outside of Egypt, but their origin is unknown.

Another surprising discovery was made near Dover, on the Kent coast, in 1992. This is also a 'sewn-plank boat', but dating slightly later, at around 1500 BCE. The section that has been reassembled and preserved is 9.5m long, although the complete boat may have been twice this size possibly.

While these discoveries do not prove that the boats are Egyptian, Phoenican or even Mycenaean, they do demonstrate the capacity for travel to the British Isles from far away, by sea-going vessels.

Returning to Ireland, Rath Navan (Navan Fort), formerly known as the important ancient site Emain Macha, was the site of an interesting find, at a place that dates back to possibly 4000 BCE. A Bronze Age structure has been discovered there, described as a roundhouse, with an attached yard and enclosure for rituals. It is thought that, at this time, the site was occupied by someone of high standing such as a king, chieftain or druid. The finds include a chape, which is a finely-decorated pin, and the skull of a Barbary ape/monkey, which was most likely a pet that was either imported or given as a gift to an important person. These monkeys (macaques) are found along the North African coast today, and may well have been common in Egypt in ancient times. A population of these apes in Tunisia was mentioned in the works of ancient Greek author Herodotus, writing in the mid 5th century BCE. The ape skull from the roundhouse has subsequently been radiocarbon dated to circa 390 - 320 BCE, placing it firmly in the Early Iron Age, nearly 1000 years after the Amarna period, but it does demonstrate trade from North Africa at a site that was important in Ireland, which had been used over thousands of years, long before the 18th Dynasty of Egypt. We can only guess when trade between Ireland and the south-eastern Mediterranean actually began, but certainly Egyptian goods arrived in Ireland from the time of the Amarna Period.

DNA Research on the Origins of the Irish and British

DNA Research was undertaken in 2015 to find any associations between the ancient Irish people and those of other countries. Some have been hoping that it would establish a definitive link with the Irish legend of Egyptian princess Meritaten, we know as Scotia or Scota.

In a joint project by by geneticists from Trinity College Dublin and archaeologists from Queen's University Belfast, evidence of massive migration to Ireland, thousands of years ago, has emerged, which came from the sequencing of the first genomes from ancient Irish humans. Sequencing the genome of an early woman farmer, who lived near Belfast some 5,200 years ago, revealed that the majority of her ancestry originated in the Middle East. The woman farmer had black hair, brown eyes and resembled southern Europeans, according to the researchers.

Also of interest was the sequencing the genomes of three men whose bodies dated from the early Bronze Age, about 4,000 years ago, showed one-third of their ancestry came from the Pontic steppe on the shores of the Black Sea. The three men, who were excavated on Rathlin Island (between the Northern Irish and Scottish coasts), had the most common Irish Y chromosome type, blue eyes and the most important variant for the genetic disease haemochromatosis, or excessive iron retention. The latter mutation is so frequent in people of Irish descent that it is sometimes referred to as a Celtic disease.

The following quote of the findings from leader of the study. Professor (of population genetics) Dan Bradley, of Trinity College Dublin, adds further insights:

"There was a great wave of genome change that swept into Europe, from above the Black Sea into Bronze Age Europe, and we now know it washed all the way to the shores of its most westerly island. And this degree of genetic change invites the possibility of other associated changes, perhaps even the introduction of language ancestral to western Celtic tongues."

Another academic involved with the project, Dr Eileen Murphy (lecturer in osteoarchaeology at Queen's University, Belfast) said the project has shown how ancient DNA analysis can provide the tools to answer such questions and that the ancient Irish genomes sequenced for the study showed "unequivocal" evidence for massive migration to Ireland.

Another member of the project, Lara Cassidy, a genetics researcher at Trinity College, Dublin said.

"Genetic affinity is strongest between the Bronze Age genomes and modern Irish, Scottish and Welsh, suggesting establishment of central attributes of the insular Celtic genome 4,000 years ago."

DNA Tests on Tutankhamun's Mummy

In 2009, extensive DNA tests were carried out on Tutankhamun's mummy and other members of his family. However, these were only partially published in February 2010. The full results of the Y-DNA test have been kept secret despite several requests for information. Researchers at Zurich-based DNA genealogy centre iGENEA, with the help of the Discovery Channel, succeeded in reconstructing the Y-DNA profile of Tutankhamun, his father Akhenaten and his grandfather Amenhotep III. The astonishing results showed that up to 70 percent of British, Irish and Spanish men are related to the Egyptian Pharaoh Tutankhamun. The study showed that half of all western European men are also related to the Egyptian Pharaoh Tutankhamun.

Tutankhamun belongs to the haplogroup R-M269. Haplogroup R-M269 originated in the region around the Black Sea about 9,500 years ago. The earliest immigration of this group to

Europe was with the spread of agriculture from 7,000 BCE, most likely there is also a strong connection with the Indo-Europeans, who spread to Europe in several waves, at a later period. It is unclear at present how the lineage of Pharaoh Thutmosis (Akenaten's and Tutankhamun's paternal ancestor) came to Egypt from the area of origin. The earliest evidence of agriculture is known from around 5000 BC, it is possible that already with the spread of agriculture from the Fertile Crescent region. Haplogroup R-M269 arrived in Egypt from the north, before the establishment of the upper and lower Egyptian kingdoms. Roman Scholz, director of the iGENEA Centre had this to say of the results:

"It was very interesting to discover that he belonged to a genetic group in Europe - there were many possible groups in Egypt that the DNA could have belonged to. We think the common ancestor lived in the Caucasus about 9,500 years ago."

So this research shows a clear genetic link with Akhenaten and Tutankhamun, but it gives not indication of the time frame of the relationship. There is most likely a common ancestor, but it is also possible that Akhenaten's descendants travelled to Spain, Britain and Ireland, the three countries that showed the highest incidence of this genome.

According to genetic studies led by Prof. Dan Bradley of Trinity College Dublin (Smurfit Institute of Genetics), Ireland's closest relatives are found in various parts of Galicia and the Basque country. He presented his research in 2009 at the American Association for the Advancement of Science annual meeting in Chicago, USA. He was joined by Prof. James Mallory of Queen's University Belfast, an archaeologist and linguist, who talked about efforts to link these DNA studies with the transmission of languages across western Europe.

The analysis of human genetic data definitively showed that the Irish have strongest relatedness with the northern Iberian Peninsula, with this genetic signal strongest for the Irish living in the west of Ireland today. These, in turn, were likely the closest relatives of the migrants who originally settled in Ireland.

Genetic studies of Irish fauna also showed this distinctive signal, Professor Bradley stated: *"The Irish badgers are Spanish, but the British badgers are not. The fauna of Ireland seems to be divergent. How does one explain this?"*

The most likely explanation was that the island was settled by migrants from northern Spain. *"It seems to me that most animals in Ireland came by boat. There seems to have been some communication with southern Europe."*

The researchers also looked for genetic linkages between people sharing a common surname, something passed along from the male lineage like the Y chromosome. They found linkages that traced back, to the famous Uí Néill kindred, of whom Niall Noigiallagh, Niall of the nine hostages, was perhaps the most well-known, and indeed a man who had definite links with Scotland. This would also explain possible links with the people of Scotland and Ireland, with those of north-western Spain - Niall of the nine hostages reputedly invaded and conquered Scotland, before military excursions into Europe, and besides, the ancestral links between Ireland and Scotland are well established.

In conclusion, there is a large body of evidence that corroborates the suggestion that there are ancient links between the Iberians and the Irish. There are also a small number of fairly recent, but conclusive, finds that link Egypt with both northern Britain and Ireland, a suggestion which would otherwise be dismissed by many as pure fantasy. These links are, of course, suggested by the Irish and Scottish annals, long regarded as 'pseudo-history', however the mass of evidence from more recent archaeology and DNA research seems to indicate that these stories are not mere fantasy in this regard, they are quite probably based on historical fact.

SCOTIA'S LEGACY

So the stories of an Egyptian princess/queen coming to Ireland are abundant, which is clear from previous chapters. Some may ask if any of this is true, if it is not just pure fantasy? In answer to that, I would suggest that these many accounts are based in truth, albeit a real history that has become partially lost, horribly distorted in some cases, mis-remembered and half-forgotten, over a huge span of time. I find it impossible to believe that so many different sources could have come up with the same 'fantasy', especially given the large body of physical and genetic evidence, that gives credence to such possibilities.

The greatest legacy of Scotia is of course the name of the country, Scotland, that is named after her tribe, the Scoti, who were supposedly the Irish descendants of her line. I say supposedly, because this is an oral tradition, in both Ireland and Scotland. There is no definitive proof of this being the case, but that is also true of many other 'tribes' that existed in Ireland in the past. I shall return to the Scoti, later in this chapter.

Local tradition, in county Kerry, maintains that Scotia died in the battle of Sliabh Mis, fought between the Milesians and the Tuatha Dé Danann, as discussed in the previous chapter. Kerry schoolchildren and Irish folklore fans may well be familiar with various versions of the story of how she fell from her horse (which also died) and how the remains of both were interred in two graves, just south of the river running through the glen. One particular story that is most certainly linked to Scotia is the story of the Stone of Destiny. While this probably can be linked in some way to the Scoti tribe, I believe it can be and should be dismissed, as factually incorrect with regard to linking Scotia personally with the Stone of Destiny/Stone of Scone. This is an interesting episode in Irish and Scottish history, but it appears to have nothing to do with Scotia herself.

Scotland's Stone of Destiny

One addendum to the story Scotia's story to consider is in regard to Scotland and its royal line, that being the story of the 'Stone of Destiny', which is also known as 'an Lia Fáil' (in the Irish language). In Scotland it is referred to as the 'Stone of Scone', where it was traditionally kept, but it is also called the 'Stone of Destiny'. The stone has been used in the crowning of Scottish kings throughout recorded history and is said to have been brought from Ireland to Scotland. The existence and origins of the stone are shrouded in mystery, but it is well-known that the Irish kings and high kings were inaugurated standing on a special stone, specifically for that purpose.

This stone has dubiously been linked with the Old Testament, also going by the alternarive name 'Jacob's Pillow'. Supposedly, it was used as a pillow by Jacob, when he had a dream of angels. According to some of the ancient texts, this stone somehow came into the possession of Gaythelos (Scotia's husband), When he was exiled from Egypt he took the stone on his long journey to Iberia and then Ireland. Other legends of Ireland suggest that it was brought to Ireland not by the Gaels but by their predecessors (who the Gaels defeated), the Tuatha Dé Danann. Even today the Lia Fáil is referred to as one of the four treasures of the Tuatha Dé Danann, brought with them to Ireland long before the arrival of the Milesians, as described in some of Ireland's ancient literature.

Figure 34: The stone at theHill of Tara, in county Meath, known as the Lia Fáil, (Photograph by Gerhard Huber).

One book that it is mentioned in is the 'Lebor Gabála Erenn' (The Book of the Taking of Ireland), although it is mentioned in several other ancient texts:

"From Failias was brought the Lia Fáil, which is in Temair (Tara), and which used to utter a cry under every king that should take Ireland. From Goirias was brought the spear which Lug had: battle

would never go against him who had it in his hand. From Findias was brought the sword of Nuadu: no man would escape from it; when it was drawn from its battle-scabbard, there was no resisting it. From Muirias was brought the cauldron of The Dagda; no company would go from it unsatisfied."

All of the Irish texts state that the Lia Fáil was brought to Ireland by the Tuatha Dé Danann, long before the Milesians arrived. The poet and Magician Morfis (also Morfessa or Fessus) from the city of Failias, one of four cities located on the northern islands of the world, where the Tuatha Dé Danann originated from:

Morfis (was) the poet of Failias itself,
In Gorias (was) Esrus of keen desires),
Semiath (was) in Murias, the fortress of pinnacles,
(And) Uscias (was) the fair seer of Findias.

Four presents (were fetched) with them hither,
By the nobles of the Tuatha Dé Danann:
A sword, a stone, a caldron of worth,
(And) a spear for the death of great champions.

From Failias (came) hither the Lia Fail,
Which shouted under the kings of Ireland.
The sword in the hand of the nimble Lug
From Gorias (it was procured), -— a choice of vast riches.

It is clear from the Irish texts that the Tuatha Dé Danann came to Ireland in a fleet of ships and settled after a war with the Fir Bolg, the indigenous people of Ireland.

Whether or not you believe Bower's account or the earlier Irish accounts, about how it got to Ireland, the stone is said to have been brought to Tara, the ancient seat of the high kings (Ard Rí) of Ireland where it resided and was used in the coronation of all Irish high kings. The link with the bible, Egypt and Spain is tenuous at best, the stone certainly existed in Ireland and perhaps it is now in Scotland, having been returned from Westminster Abbey in England.

According to the late Professor Daithi Ó Hogain:

"The myth of Connaire states that the two steeds of one colour, never before harnessed, were placed under a chariot and that they could only be controlled by the man destined to be king. A special mantle fitted only the true king, whose selection had further to be ratified by a vision of seers (druids). When the chariot was driven by that man, two flagstones at Tara would open before it to allow it through and the upright stone call Lia Fíal screeched against its axle."

Other accounts of the stone state that the would-be high king was obliged to stand on the stone, whereupon the stone would screech out in recognition of that man being the true and rightful high king of Ireland. Today a rather phallic stone is to be found at Tara, on the most westerly of two intersecting mounds known as 'An Forradh' and 'Teach Cormaic'. The stone stands upright on the former. Interestingly, the stone is impractical as something that a king might stand on, which begs the question - is it the original stone? Other such stones, used for regional coronations (such as the kings of Leinster) were known to be oblong in shape and suitable for someone to stand upon. It seems odd, to me at least, that the 'Lia Fáil' at Tara is a completely different shape.

Dál Riada, the Scots and The Stone of Destiny

In legend it is said that the stone was brought to Scotland from Ireland by king Fergus Mór (Fergus the great) circa 498 CE. However, it is also linked with other Irish kings - Muirchertach mac Muiredaig (Mac Ercae) who lived circa 470- 534 CE and the famous Niall Noígíallach (Niall of the Nine Hostages) who reigned around 368–395 CE, although this time period is disputed by the various Irish texts. Niall, who I mentioned earlier, was the progenitor of the Uí Néill dynasty, that to a huge extent dominated Ireland, up until the 10th century CE.

The people who the Romans referred to as Scoti were different people from the indigenous Picti (or Picts) of Scotland, the

Figure 35: The Stone of Destiny is also known as the Stone of Scone, and is also referred to as The Coronation Stone (in England). This block of red sandstone was used for centuries during the coronation of Scottish kings. After its theft, it was used during the coronation of English and British monarchs (held in Perth Museum. Public domain photograph).

Scoti came from Ireland. The Scoti were involved in the raids on Britain, possibly throughout the Roman occupation, and they were most certainly involved in the 'Barbarian Conspiracy' of 367 CE, when Roman Britain was overwhelmed by the combined forces of Scoti, Picts, Angles and Saxons, attacking at the same time.

When the Scoti first began settling in Scotland is unknown, but it is known that they were raiding the Hebrides (Scottish islands), the Welsh coast and western mainland of Britain in the centuries before the 'Barbarian Conspiracy'. The oldest mention of the migration of the Scoti, into what is now Scotland, appears to come from 'Senchus fer n-Alban' (Traditions/Laws of the Men of Scotland) which is an Irish text dating from the 7th century CE. This account mentions king Fergus Mór Mac Eirc coming from Antrim (north west Ireland) and settling in Argyll (western Scotland), presumably bringing the 'Lia Fáil', or Stone of Destiny, with him.

Fergus is not a widely remembered ruler in Ireland, but Niall Noígíallach (also credited with bringing the 'Lia Fáil' to Scotland) is well known, to this day.

There are a great many accounts of his life, but according to the saga 'The Death of Niall of the Nine Hostages', Niall made war in Europe as far as the Alps, and the Romans sent an ambassador to negotiate with him. Rather abruptly, the tale then has Niall appearing before an assembly of Pictish bards in Scotland, where he was killed by an arrow. The arrow was sent by a longstanding enemy Eochaid (son of Leinster king Énnae Cennsalach), from the other side of the valley. Niall, along with Fergus is given as progenitor of the kingdom of Dál Riada, which was established in Scotland, as early as the 4th century CE, perhaps even earlier. The Scottish line of kings, down even to the Stuarts, claim ancestry from Dál Riada and even back to the Scoti and their legendary ancestors Scotia and Gaythelos.

There is also a story of how the Irish monk and missionary Saint Columba (Colmcille) brought the stone to the Isle of Iona, in the 6th century CE, thus we can see at least four possibilities, according to ancient texts, of how the stone was brought to Scotland.

The 9th century CE saw Kenneth MacAlpin (who reigned circa 841 - 859 CE) bringing the stone (also called Clach-na Cinneamhuinn) to what is now Scone Abbey, where he was crowned upon it. It is suggested that Scone was an important site since the early 8th century CE, as a Christian religious site of the Culdees (Céli Dé meaning 'Companions of God'). Presumably the stone arrived in Scotland in the 4th or 5th century CE and resided at Scone since MacAplin's reign, but the abbey itself, which later housed the stone, was established around 1114 CE. From the coronation of Kenneth MacAlpin onwards, all the Scottish kings were crowned on the stone at Scone up until 1296 CE.

At his coronation in 1249 CE, the Scottish King Alexander III heard his royal genealogy recited back through 56 generations back to Scotia. It was also accepted that the 'Stone of Destiny', the flat rock upon which Kings of Scotland (and thereafter Britain) were crowned, had been brought over from Egypt by Scotia.

In 1286 CE, Alexander III of Scotland (r. 1249-1286 CE) died, leaving his infant granddaughter as his successor - Margaret the 'Maid of Norway'. It was agreed by the Scottish nobles that she would be queen of Scotland, however, on her voyage from Norway to Scotland, she unfortunately died, at the tender age of seven. There were subsequently thirteen claimants to the Scottish throne, and the Scots asked Edward I of England to act as mediator. A Scots noble (one of the thirteen), John Baliol, was chosen as the new king of Scotland and crowned at Scone, but many Scots resented Edward's interference in their government, and rebelled. John Baliol formed an alliance with the French in 1296 CE and fought against the English. but Baliol lost a critical battle at Dunbar in April 1296 CE.

It is known that King Edward I of England took the stone in 1296 CE. during his invasion and occupation of Scotland. He had it removed to Westminster Abbey in London, where it was fitted into a wooden chair – known as King Edward's Chair, or as The Coronation Chair. This was an attempt to usurp the authority of the Scottish line of kings, in his attempts to conquer Scotland. It was on this chair that most of the subsequent English and then British sovereigns have been crowned. Charles III of England (officially of Great Britain and Northern Ireland) was crowned on this chair, but the stone itself (66 cm × 42 cm × 27 cm weighing approximately 152 kg was previously returned to Scotland briefly when it was stolen by Scottish nationalists led by Ian Hamilton, a student at the University of Glasgow, in 1950.

In 1996, the stone was returned to Scotland on a permanent basis, in November of that year. There was a formal ceremony at the border of Scotland and England, transferring the stone back to the care of Scotland. and initially it was kept in Edinburgh castle. However, the stone remains property of the British

Crown, and is transported to London for use at coronations, most recently it was used at the coronation of king Charles III at Westminster Abbey. Since March 2024, the Stone of Destiny has been returned and is now on permanent public display at Perth, in eastern Scotland.

The legend connecting Scotia to the Stone of Destiny and its transfer to Scotland did not appear in any known books until the early 14th century CE, it is thought that its mention was given in order to increase the significance of the Scottish people's history and show an ancient heritage going back to ancient Egypt.

The Declaration of Arbroath

This story which is well established in myth, in what is described as 'pseudo-histories' became a very real part of actual history, when this version of Scottish lineage was cited to reaffirm the cause of independence and sovereignty for the Scottish people. This lineage in the 'Declaration of Arbroath', was given because of the events of the preceding century, particularly the invasion by Edward I of England.

The 'Declaration of Arbroath' was an important letter/document written by Scottish Barons and Noblemen in 1320 CE, which was addressed to Pope John XXII, and was sent to explain and defend the position taken by the Scots, during their war of independence against England. It constituted the position of King Robert I (Robert the Bruce) in response to his excommunication from the Church, for disobeying the Pope's demand in 1317 CE for a truce in the First War of Scottish Independence.

The document, written in Latin, explains the glorious lineage and journey of the descendants of Princess Scotia from ancient lands to that of Scotland. It explains how the ancestors of the Scottish people faced inhospitable terrain and hostile people, but surrendered to no-one and always came out victorious over their adversaries, thus making them inferior to none and hence suitable to determine their own affairs themselves and thus confirm their own sovereignty. The Scottish Declaration of Independence (Declaration of Arbroath, 1320 CE), translated from the original Latin, is as follows:

"To the Most Saintly Father in Christ the Lord, the Lord John, by divine Providence, Supreme Pontiff of the Holy Roman Catholic Church, from his humble and devoted sons, Duncan - Earl of Fife, Thomas Ranulph - Earl of Moray, Lord of Man and Annandale, Patrick Dunbar - Earl of March, Malise - Earl of Strathearn, Malcolm - Earl of Leven, William - Earl of Ross, Magnus - Earl of Caithness and Orkney, and William - Earl of Sutherland; Walter - Seneschal of Scotland, William Soules - Butler of Scotland, James - Lord of Douglas, Roger Mowbray, David - Lord of Brechin, David Graham, Ingram Umfraville, John Menteith - Guardian of the Earldom of Menteith, Alexander Fraser, Gibert Hay - Constable of Scotland, Robert Keith - Marischal of Scotland, Henry Sinclair, John Graham, David Lindsay, William Olifaunt, Patrick Graham, John Fentoun, William Abernethy, David Wemys, William Montefix, Fergus Ardrossan, Eustace Maxwell, William Ramsay, William Montealt, Alan Moray, Donald Campbell, John Cameron, Reginald leChien, Alexander Setoun, Andrew Leslie, and Alexander Stratoun, along with the other Barons, Freeholders and all the common people of the kingdom of Scotland, we send every filial reverence with devoted kisses of your blessed feet.

Most Holy Father and Lord, we know from the deeds of the ancients and we read from books -- because among the other great nations of course, our nation of Scots has been described in many publications -- that crossing from Greater Scythia, via the Tyrhennian Sea and the Pillars of Hercules, and living in Spain among the fiercest tribes for many years, it could be conquered by no one anywhere, no matter how barbarous the tribes. Afterwards, coming from there, one thousand two hundred years from the Israelite people's crossing of the Red Sea, to its home in the west, which it now holds, having first thrown out the Britons and completely destroyed the Picts, and even though it was often attacked by the Norse, the Danes and the English, it fought back with many victories and countless labours and it has held itself ever since, free from all slavery, as the historians of old testify. In their own kingdom, one hundred and thirteen kings have reigned of their own Blood Royal, without interruption by foreigners.

The merits and nobility of these people, even if they were not obvious from the other signs, shine out openly enough from this, that even though they lived at the furthermost ends of the Earth, the King of kings and the Lord of lords, Jesus Christ after His Passion and His Resurrection, called them nearly the first to his most Holy Faith. Nor did He want to confirm them in the said Faith by anyone but the first to be an Apostle, despite being second or third in rank, the brother of the Blessed Peter, gentle Saint Andrew, whom ever since, He has asked to protect them as their Patron.

However, the Holy Fathers, your predecessors, considering these thoughts with a careful mind, bestowed on this very kingdom and people many favours and countless privileges since it was the special charge of Blessed Peter's brother. Thus, obviously, the result *was that until now our people lived free and untroubled under their protection until that mighty prince, Edward, King of the English, the father of he who now reigns, came with the appearance of a friend and ally to harass like an enemy, our leaderless kingdom and our people who were accustomed neither to evil or treachery nor to battles or ambushes. He committed injustices, killings, attacks,*

Figure 36: The only existing copy of the Declaration-of-Arbroath (held in the Scottish National Archives, Edinburgh. Public domain photograph)

robberies, arson, the imprisonment of priests, the burning of monasteries, the looting of churches, and countless other enormous outrages, on the said people sparing no one on account of age or sex, saintliness or rank, to an extent that no one could describe nor fully believe except one who had experienced it.

From these countless evils, with His help who afterwards soothes and heals wounds, we are freed by our tireless leader, king, and master, Lord Robert, who like another Maccabaeus or Joshua, underwent toil and tiredness, hunger and danger with a light spirit in order to free the people and his inheritance from the hands of his enemies. And now, the divine Will, our just laws and customs, which we will defend to the death, the right of succession and the due consent and assent of all of us have made him our leader and our king. To this man, inasmuch as he saved our people, and for upholding our freedom, we are bound by right as much as by his merits, and choose to follow him in all that he does.

But if he should cease from these beginnings, wishing to give us or our kingdom to the English or the king of the English, we would immediately take steps to drive him out as the enemy and the subverter of his own rights and ours, and install another King who would make good our defence. Because, while a hundred of us remain alive, we will not submit in the slightest measure, to the domination of the English. We do not fight for honour, riches, or glory, but solely for freedom which no true man gives up but with his life.

It is for these reasons, Reverend Father and Lord, that we beg your holiness with humble hearts and every urgent prayer, knowing that you will review everything with a true heart and a saintly mind since before Him in Whose name you reign on Earth there is neither bias nor difference between Jeudaean or Greek, Scot or Angle, and considering with paternal eyes the trouble and anguish brought on us and the Church of God by the English, that you will warn the king of the English, that he ought to be satisfied with what he owns because once it used to be enough for seven kings, and that you will think it right to encourage him to leave us Scots in peace, living in poor Scotland beyond which there is nothing habitable and nothing we desire. For this, we will effectively do whatever we can to gain peace, bearing in mind our situation.

For this concerns you, Holy Father, since you see the raging ferocity of the pagans against Christians, which the sins of the Christians deserve, and the borders of Christendom being pushed back every day and you must see how much it will hurt your saintly reputation, if (which let it not) any part of the church be overcome or induced to sin during your time. Therefore let Him rouse those Christian leaders who say that they cannot go in support of the Holy Land for no reason although they pretend that the reason is wars with their neighbours. The reason for their difficulties is actually because they expect better rewards and weaker resistance in warring with their smaller neighbours. But the omniscient One knows well enough with how light a heart we and our aforesaid lord and king would go there, if the king of the English would leave us in peace. This we declare and testify to Christ's vicar and to all Christendom.

If your Holiness, trusting too much in the English version of these events, does not truly believe us, or does not stop supporting them to our disadvantage, then, we believe that the slaughter of bodies, the loss of souls, and all the other things that will follow, the injuries that they will do to us and we to them, will be blamed by the Most High on you.

Thus, as if your sons, we are and always will be ready to do for you, His vicar, whatever you require insofar as it is our duty; and so, we commit the upholding of our cause to the Supreme King and Judge, entrusting our worries to Him and completely confident that He will fill us with courage and reduce our enemies to nothing.

May God grant you holiness and health in His holy church for a long time.

Sent from the Monastery of Arbroath in Scotland, on the 6th day of the month April, in the year of Grace 1320, the fifteenth year of our above mentioned king's reign."

The original copy of the declaration, that was sent to Avignon, is lost. The only existing manuscript copy of the declaration survives among Scotland's state papers, measuring 540mm wide by 675mm long (including the seals) and is currently held at the National Archives of Scotland (NAS) in Edinburgh.

So, after an exploration of the origins of Scotia and her previous life as Meritaten, once princess and queen of Egypt, we see that her story has had an enormous impact on the history of Spain and in particular both Scotland and Ireland. For a woman who existed in the 14th century BCE, her legendary exploits and her influence reverberates through history, down to our current time.

Her name can be found associated with the sovereignty and fight for independence of both Ireland and Scotland, a name that has been wielded with great pride. We have little idea of what she actually looked like, other than the Egyptian busts made during her lifetime, but these are probably highly stylised.

Irish political cartoonist John Fergus O'Hea (circa 1838 – 1922),

Queen. Scota unfur's the Sacred Banner.

Figure 37: John Fergus O'Hea's illustration entitled 'Queen Scotia Unfurls The Sacred Banner'(Public domain photograph).

who sometimes published under the pseudonym 'Spex', produced one of the most iconic modern images of Scotia, although we can be certain that she looked nothing like the woman he depicted. O'Hea was active in the Young Ireland movement and had been secretary to Daniel O'Connell, known in his time as 'The Liberator' and the acknowledged political leader of Ireland's campaign for the emancipation of the Roman Catholic majority.

Ultimately O'Connell failed to achieve either the repeal of the 1800 CE Act of Union or the restoration of the Irish Parliament. However, even if O'Hea is not well remembered, his friend Daniel O'Connell certainly is, as is the famed Scotia, who he depicted in the late 1800s. The image he created is rather fanciful and based on romantic ideas of the time, it was designed to stir up patriotism among the oppressed Irish people, who were still under the yoke of the British Empire.

A quick search of the names Scotia or Scota reveals myriad articles and mentions of her across the internet, many of them ill-informed. However, one can see that she is still a part of modern consciousness. Living in Kerry for many years, I am well aware that local people, even school children know who Scotia was, and are rightly proud that she is part of Irish heritage and culture.

Likewise in Scotland, many are aware that the name of their country has its origins in her name and the tribe (Scoti) who were presumably descended from her family. Her legacy is immense for someone who lived some 3300 or more years ago. Like her younger brother, Tutankhamun, she has become a popular icon, although most do not connect the two people. I personally believe that Scotia was Meritaten, based on the evidence from five different countries. Certainly there is a mass of evidence to suggest that

Meritaten, the eldest daughter of Pharaoh Akhenaten and the older half-sister of his only son Tutankhamun, is the person who later came to be known as Scotia, or Scota.

What I have presented in this book connects the dots of Meritaten's life with that of the mythical Scotia, but the evidence is not 100% conclusive. The evidence shows the possibility and the high likelihood that these events, described in the Irish and Scottish texts, are based on reality. In order to prove that Scotia was Meritaten, or any of the daughters of Akhenaten, it would be necessary to excavate Scotia's Grave. If indeed a corpse was found at Scotia's Grave (Leac Scoitín) DNA samples could be taken, in order to analyse the origin of the person. As was done with the mummies of Akhenaten and Tutankhamun, a DNA comparison would be vital to prove any relationship between any person buried at Scotia's Grave and both Akhenaten and Tutankhamun.

This is the final 'piece of the puzzle' so to speak, and until the site is excavated there will not, and cannot, be any indisputable proof that Meritaten is Scotia/Scota, or that she came to Ireland. If a body was found and a DNA analysis was done and a paternal and sibling link was established beyond doubt, then it would prove that the stories, often dismissed as 'pseudo-history', are based (however loosely) on historical events.

Currently there are no plans that I am aware of to investigate Scotia's Grave further, but I am hopeful that this may change in the future. Excavation could be the key to providing conclusive answers about the validity of both the Egyptian and Hittite texts regarding the Amarna royal family and also the much later Spanish, Irish and Scottish legends about Scotia.

BIBLIOGRAPHY

Ahlstrom, Dick - Genetic studies show our closest relatives are found in Galicia and the Basque region (Irish Times, 2009)

Alred, Cyril – Akhenaten, King of Egypt (Thames & Hudson, 1988)

Belzoni, Giovani Battista - Narrative of the operations and recent discoveries within the pyramids, temples, tombs, and excavations, in Egypt and Nubia; and of a journey to the coast of the Red Sea, in search of the ancient Berenice, and of another to the oasis of Jupiter Ammon (J. Murray, 1820)

Best, R. I. - The Settling of the Manor of Tara, Eiru Vol 4 (Royal Irish Academy, 1910)

Bower, Walter, edited by Watt, D.E.R - A History Book for Scots: Selections from the Scotichronicon (Mercat Press, 1998)

Calder, George (Tr.) - Auraicept na n-Éces: The Scholar's Primer (John Grant, 1917)

Carter, Howard - The Tomb of Tutankhamen (Cassell, 1923)

Collyer, Alec - Archaeologists make incredible Bronze Age discovery in National Park (BBC, 2024)

Cullen, Paul - Ancient Irish had Middle Eastern ancestry, study reveals (Irish Times, 2015)

Draper-Stumm, Tara - Sekhmet Statues From the Reign of Amenhotep III in the British Museum and a Formerly Uncatalogued Head Fragment: A Reassessment (Cambridge University Press, 2018)

Duffy, Seán - Crowning of Ireland's Last, Scottish High King (Irish Times, 2015)

Ellis, Ralph - Scota, Egyptian Queen of Scots (Edfu Books, 2006)

Eleazar, Alexandre - Los Bere (Gráficas Instar, 1985)

Evans, Lorraine - Kingdom of the Ark: That Startling Story of How the Ancient British Race is Descended from the Pharaohs (Simon & Schuster Ltd. 2000)

Faulkner, Raymond O = A Concise Dictionary of Middle Egyptian (Oxford University Press, 1962)

Goren, Y., Finkelstein, I. & Na'aman, N. -Inscribed in Clay – Provenance Study of the Amarna Tablets and Other Ancient Near Eastern Texts, from The Emery and Clare Yass Publications in Archaeology Monograph Series No. 23 (Institute of Archaeology of Tel Aviv University, 2004)

Gerson, Livia - Ancient City's Destruction by Exploding Space Rock May Have Inspired Biblical Story of Sodom (Smithsonian Magazine, 2021)

Gertoux, Gérard - Scientific approach to an absolute chronology through synchronisms dated by astronomy (Université Lumiere Lyon, 2019)

Greenhouse, Molly - Investigating the "Sea Peoples": Nomadic tribes and causes of migration from Anatolia in the Late Bronze Age (USC School of Architecture, 2012)

HARTIS, Integrated Nautical Services - The Bronze Age and the Sophisticated Ships of the Minoans (Hartis.org, 2017)

Hull, Vernam - The Four Jeweles of the Tuatha Dé Danann. ZCP. vol. XVIII. NY (G.E. Stechert Co. 1930)

IGENEA - Are you a direct male descendant of the pharaohs? iGENEA exclusively publishes the Y-DNA profile of Tutankhamun and searches for his last living relatives (igenea. com, 2011)

Hogg, Ulrike and MacGregor, Martin - Written and Unwritten Pasts: Scottish Historiography in Highlands and Lowlands, 1400-1650 (University of Glasgow, 2019)

John of Fordun - Chronica Gentis Scotorum, edited and translated by Skene, William. F. (H.M. General Register House, 1867)

Jones, Dr. Alfred - Tampering with the Chariot (article: Historic Mysteries, 2010)

Keating, Geoffrey - The General History of Ireland, edited and translated by Dermod O'Connor (B. Creake, 1723)

Kinsella, Eoin Dr. (Ed.) - Dictionary of Irish Biography (Royal Irish Academy, 2009-24)

Kotch, John T. & Carey James - The Celtic Heroic Age: Literary Sources for Ancient Celtic Europe & Early Ireland & Wales (Celtic Studies Publications, 2003)

Magnusson, Magnus - Scotland, the Story of a Nation (HarperCollins, 2000)

Marie, Mustafa - Recent excavations in Spain's Salamanca uncovers amulets belonging to Egyptian deity Hathor (Egypt Today, 2021)

Martin, Geoffrey T. – The Royal Tomb at El-'Amarna Vol 1 (Egypt Exploration Society, 1974)

Mosenkis, Iurii - Hellenic Origin of Europe (PP Zhovtyi O. O., 2016)

Mosenkis, Iurii - Minoan Greek Traders in Norway (Academia, 2016)

Moriarty, Colm - A Barbary Ape Skull from Navan Fort, Co. Armagh (Irish Archaeology, 2014)

Murnane, William J. - Texts from the Amarna Period in Egypt (Scholars Press, 1995)

Ó Flaherty, Roderick - Ogygia, or a Chronological Account of Irish Events (Collected from Very Ancient Documents Faithfully Compared with Each Other & Supported by the Genealogical & Chronological Aid of the Sacred and Profane Writings of the Globe), edited and translated by Rev. James Hely (W. MacKenzie, 1793)

Ó Hogan, Dr. Daithi – Myth Legend and Romance (BCA, 1990)

MacAlister, R.A. Stewart - Lebor Gabála Erenn (Irish Texts Society, 1942)

Ramos, Teodoro Fondón - Egypt, the Mediterranean Sea and the Iberian Peninsula in Antiquity (arqueogestion.com, 2019)

Sainero, Ramón - The Celtic origins of the kingdom of Brigantia. The genesis of Spain (Los orígenes celtas del reino de Brigantia: la génesis de España), Ed. Abada (Abada Editores, 2009)

Sainero, Ramón - The Celtic footprint in Spain and Ireland (La

Huella Celta En Espana E Irlanda), Ed. Akal (Akal Ediciones, 1987)

Science Daily - After 5,000 Year Voyage, World's Oldest Built Boats Deliver -- Archeologists' First Look Confirms Existence Of Earliest Royal Boats At Abydos (New York University, 2000)

Simpson, William Kelly - The Literature of Ancient Egypt: An Anthology of Stories, Instructions, and Poetry (Yale University Press, 2003)

Santini, Valentina - Enquiry on Meritaten: The Many Aspects of an Exceptional Amarna Woman, in Journal of the Hellenic Institute of Egyptology (Serapis Editions, 2021)

Teryan, Angela - Ancient Written Sources of the European Nations About Their Ancenstral Homeland - Armenia and Armenians (Voskan Yerevantsi, 2017)

Van der Crabben, Jan - World History Encyclopaedia (World History Encyclopaedia, 2009-24)

Wachsmann, Shelley - Seagoing Ships & Seamanship in the Bronze Age Levant (Texas A&M University Press, 1998)

William, R. Alans & Le Carlier de Veslud, Cécile - Boom and bust in Bronze Age Britain: major copper production from the Great Orme mine and European trade, c. 1600–1400 BC, in Antiquity, A Review of World Archeology (Cambridge University, 2019)

Winkley, Cassandra L. - The Production and Perception of Bronze in Mycenaean Greece (The University of Texas at Austin, 2020)

Woolf, Alex, "Senchus Fer n-Alban", in: John T. Koch (ed.), Celtic culture: a historical encyclopedia, volume 4 (Bloomsbury Academic, 2006)